REPRESENTING THE OTHER?

Representing the Other?

SANSKRIT SOURCES AND THE MUSLIMS

Eighth to Fourteenth Century

BRAJADULAL CHATTOPADHYAYA

PRIMUS
BOOKS

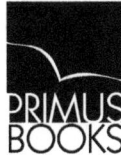

PRIMUS BOOKS
An imprint of Ratna Sagar P. Ltd.
Virat Bhavan
Mukherjee Nagar Commercial Complex
Delhi 110 009

Offices at CHENNAI LUCKNOW
AGRA AHMEDABAD BENGALURU COIMBATORE DEHRADUN GUWAHATI HYDERABAD
JAIPUR JALANDHAR KANPUR KOCHI KOLKATA MADURAI MUMBAI PATNA
RANCHI VARANASI

Reprinted 2017

ISBN: 978-93-86552-07-5 (hardback)
ISBN: 978-93-86552-36-5 (POD)
ISBN: 978-93-86552-08-2 (paperback)
ISBN: 978-93-86552-09-9 (e-book)

Published by Primus Books

Lasertypeset by Sai Graphic Design
Arakashan Road, Paharganj, New Delhi 110 055

Printed and bound in India by Replika Press Pvt. Ltd.

Dedicated,

in humility,

to the memories of

ABDUL KARIM KHAN

ALAUDDIN KHAN

BUNDU KHAN

FAIYAZ KHAN

SAWAI GANDHARVA

Contents

Preface

What is being published as a short monograph was originally intended to be worked out in the form of an essay. However, as research and writing on the theme of this work progressed, I came to feel that brevity can be a virtue only of the brave; for me, it was necessary to have enough space to be able to incorporate relevant primary material, in order to present an understanding of the possible meanings embedded in the material, and to submit an argument. I did not feel bold enough to be brief. This diffidence will also account for the lengthy quotations, from sources as well as from their interpreters, with which my text is interspersed. They are there to let others judge how wildly astray I may have gone in my grasp of their meanings.

Let me clarify two points. One, the title of the work is somewhat inconsistent with what one will come across in the text. The Sanskrit sources do not deliberately 'represent'; representation is our device imposed on the sources, but it does perhaps help us understand the sources. Further, if Sanskrit sources do not refer to one, unified, homogenous Muslim community, then is the use of the term 'Muslim' justified in the title of a work which seeks to examine only such sources? However, use of possible alternatives like Yavana, Mleccha, Śaka, Turuṣka—terms which were being regularly used in sources of early medieval/medieval period—does not really offer a viable solution; then, how does one, historiographically, distinguish between early Yavanas or Śakas and those of the later periods?

The second point is that the present work is not about relations between Hindus and Muslims in the early medieval/medieval period. I do not feel competent to deal with such a theme, at least to my own satisfaction. The monograph examines only one category of source—literary and epigraphic texts which share some similarities—in order to find out how well they convey to us general attitudes to groups of newcomers to Indian society in various capacities, from a certain period of time. The sources can at best be used to understand one perspective, that of those familiar with literate conventions and modes of their transmission. Even they may not correspond to one perspective, and one would therefore be justified in assuming the existence of others. This exercise is therefore in a way a critique of attempts to construct collective consciousnesses of the past by putting absolute trust on written evidence, which itself, on inspection, may be found susceptible to equivocation. History, one has to admit, is constructed with reference to the present, but it can be done by sparing the past an identity with or proximity to a single strand in our contemporary consciousness. Past, simply as past, is an a historical notion; the burden of our current malaise therefore cannot simply and conveniently be passed off to any past, in any way we choose.

The idea of writing on the theme of the present work stemmed from my general interest in the history of early medieval India and has been with me for the past several years. I even got an M.Phil. student of mine, Anwar Hussain, to write an M.Phil. thesis for the Centre for Historical Studies, Jawaharlal Nehru University, on an aspect of this theme a few years back. However, my own work on it could begin only recently. Fifteen days of uninterrupted work in Paris, in July 1995, made possible by the authorities of the Maison des Sciences de L'Homme helped me formulate the initial plan of the work. The work itself was carried out in Leipzig in the summer of 1996, and that it finally took some shape is practically due to Professor Bernhard Kölver, Director of the Institut für Indologie und Zentralasienwissenschaften at Universitat Leipzig. Professor Kölver went out of his way to arrange, by securing generous financial resources from the German Research Council, a one-year Visiting Professorship for me tenable at the University of Leipzig. I do not hesitate to confess that but for this offer from the German Research Council and the facilities made readily available at the University of Leipzig, it would have taken me much longer to bring the contemplated work to its present shape.

The completion of this work owes a great deal to the help and encouragement of several friends and colleagues. Professor Hermann Kulke who holds the Chair of Asian History at the University of Kiel was most generous in making photocopies of material required for the work available and in sparing his precious time in not only commenting on my first draft but also, along with his wife, being a fastidious host during our stay in Kiel. Dr Maria Schetelich of the Institute at Leipzig introduced to me texts I had not come across before and made life in Leipzig easy for us despite our linguistic ignorance. I was fortunate also to have easy access to Dr Mahes Raj Pant's versatility in Sanskrit and to the expertise of other colleagues at the Leipzig Institute. While I am grateful to all individuals mentioned here, I alone remain responsible for the views that I have expressed.

Centre for Historical Studies
Jawaharlal Nehru University

BRAJADULAL CHATTOPADHYAYA

CHAPTER 1

The Twin Burdens: Historiography and Sources

The Burden of Historiography

The history of how 'others' were perceived and represented in the past in India has hardly been conscientiously worked upon by historians so far,[1] although clear assumptions regarding such perception and representation have been strongly entrenched in Indological studies, since, perhaps their inception. These assumptions continue to dominate, without adequate and fresh references to primary sources, our own understandings of India's past, and one finds that in the matter of reinforcing assumptions regarding the 'others' of the past, different strands of historical thinking—be they Imperialist, 'Orientalist', National or of other categories—curiously seem to converge. This is indeed curious, since, for example, while for the Orientalists, the Indian culture, as a segment of the Oriental culture, may represent the other, the prerogative, at the same time, of defining the other within this otherness of India was appropriated also by the Orientalists. One example of this is the accentuated dichotomy between the Aryan and the non-Aryan,[2]

[1] Two notable exceptions are: Romila Thapar, 'The Image of the Barbarian in Early India', *Comparative Studies in Society and History*, vol. 13, 1971, pp. 408–36; Aloka Parasher, *Mlecchas in Early India: A Study in Attitudes towards Outsiders upto AD 600*, Delhi, 1991.

[2] Bibliographies of recent works, indicating continuity of concerns about Aryan origins, will be found in R.S. Sharma, *Looking for the Aryans*, Hyderabad, 1994; G. Erdosy, ed., *The Indo-Aryans of Ancient South Asia: Language. Material Culture and Ethnicity*, Berlin, New York, 1995. For brief comments on the link between theories on the Aryans and

which continues to haunt Indian historical writings. Equally, or perhaps more, critical, particularly for the purpose of what we intend to investigate in this monograph, are the implications of the periodization of pre-'British' Indian history into Hindu and Muslim.[3] This schema of periodization has implications, such as construction of homogenous politico-cultural entities which are, by nature, changeless and can be antagonistic to other similarly homogeneous, changeless politico-cultural entities.[4] These, and similar other implications, await rigorous identification and analysis. However, scrutiny, even at a superficial level, suggests that the schema underscored, in a very clear fashion, how the boundary of the 'otherness' was to be defined. The boundary relates to both history and culture—to how the end and beginning

---

the ideology of imperialism, see Thomas R. Metcalf, *Ideologies of the Raj*, The New Cambridge History of India, III.4, Cambridge, 1995, Chap. 3.

[3] James Mill to whom is attributed the scheme of periodization (Romila Thapar, 'Interpretations of Ancient Indian History', in *Ancient Indian Social History: Some Interpretations*, Delhi, 1978, pp. 1–25) has a curious assessment of the nature of 'Muslim rule' in India: 'The conquest of Hindustan, effected by the Mohammedan nations, was to no extra-ordinary degree sanguinary or destructive. It substituted sovereigns of one race to sovereigns of another; and mixed with the old inhabitants a small proportion of new; but it altered not the texture of society, it altered not the language of the country the original inhabitants remained the occupants of the soil; they continued to be governed by their own laws and institutions; nay, the whole detail of administration, with the exception of the army, and a few of the more prominent situations, remained invariably in the hands of the native magistrates and offices. The few occasions of persecution, to which, under the reigns of one or two bigoted sovereigns, they were subjected on the score of religion, were too short and too partial to produce any considerable effects.' James Mill, *The History of British India*, vol. I, 1817, Delhi; repr. 1978, pp. 461–2. Yet, Mill stresses the dichotomy of two civilizations in the context of Indian History: Hindu and Muslim, and remarks: 'The question, therefore, is whether by a government moulded and conducted agreeably to the properties of Persian civilization, instead of government moulded and conducted agreeably to the properties of Hindu civilization, the Hindu population of India lost or gained'; ibid., p. 700. Mill was in no doubt about the distinctiveness and relative qualities of what he considered two nations and two civilizations: 'it is necessary to ascertain, as exactly as possible, the particular stage of civilization at which these nations had arrived. . . . It is requisite for the purpose of ascertaining whether the civilization of the Hindus received advancement of depression, from the ascendancy over them which the Mohammedans acquired'; ibid., Chap. 15. The equation of civilization with race and religion is implicit in Mill's comments.

[4] For a recent review see Barbara D. Metcalf, 'Presidential Address: Too Little and Too Much: Reflections on Muslims in The History of India', *The Journal of Asian Studies*, vol. 54, no. 4, 1995, pp. 951–67.

of periods of history were to be considered, and how cultural lines could be prevented from overlapping.[5]

To an extent, the schema and the underlying assumption regarding periodization were derived from an insistence upon a unitary vision, marginalizing regional specificities and thereby putting forward generalizations for Indian history.[6] The periodization schema and the associated characterizations of periods therefore continue to be adopted and used by historians, writing on India, or on a region as its component, even when history writing has departed very substantially from the context in which the schema originated. One can demonstrate this continuity by referring to a wide range of writings—from school textbooks through Nationalist to post-Nationalist analyses of what may be called the twilight zone, in historiography, of 'pre-medieval-medieval' juncture of Indian history. While the terms Hindu and Muslim may not continue to be used in the context of periodization, by and large the notion of 'Hindu'-'Muslim' divide remains the implicit major boundaryline, separating one Indian past from the other, and thereby marginalizing the continuity, interaction and modification of cultural elements in history. It is not the intention of this work to go into historiography in any detail. Nevertheless, the point about the persistent image of politico-cultural dichotomy, and of the streotypical perception of the 'other', needs to be established by referring to particular

[5] Although 'nationalist' historiographical agenda is believed to have been set in motion by challenging Orientalist notions, the nationalists themselves adopted the essential Orientalist premises and methods for writing about their country's past. Partha Chatterjee has shown recently how big the difference between Mrityunjay Vidyalankar's *Rājāvalī*, written for the use of young officials of the East India Company in Calcutta in 1808, and Tarinicharan Chattopadhyaya's *Bharatvarsher Itihas* (first published in 1858) is. While Vidyalankar's text can be considered a 'Puranik History', Chattopadhyaya's history of the country informed by colonial historiography of the period, has a striking opening: 'India (*Bhāratavarṣa*) has been ruled in turn by Hindus. Muslims and Christians. Accordingly, the history of this country (*deś*) is divided into the periods of Hindu, Muslim and Christian rule (*rājatva*).' Partha Chatterjce, 'Claims on the Past: The Genealogy of Modern Historiography in Bengal', in *Subaltern Studies VIII: Essays in Honour of Ranijit Guha, ed.* David Arnold and David Hardiman, Delhi, 2nd ptg., 1995, pp. 1–49.

[6] Antagonism to regional history is articulated clearly: 'It [regional history] gives, if we may so express ourselves, a sort of double plot to the history; and what is worse, it renders the grand plot subservient to the little one. The object too is not, in our opinion, worthy of the sacrifice.' Quoted without appropriate reference in 'Preface', M.D. Hussain, *A Study of Nineteenth Century Historical works on Muslim Rule in Bengal: Charles Stewart to Henry Beveridge*, Dhaka, 1987. Whether it is a question of political sovereignty or of culture, total neglect of localities and regions not only blurs our vision of ground-level patterns but also hinders our understanding of the 'grand plot' itself.

works of history, precisely dated and therefore evidence of the authentication of assumptions, held as valid at precise chronological points of their articulation. In arguing about the persistence of historiographical premises, I start by citing the Foreword in the fourth volume of a well-known series, which is in regular use among students in Indian universities and to which contributions came from the best available experts in the field. K.M. Munshi, in his Foreword to *The Age of Imperial Kanauj* (vol. 4 of *The History and Culture of the Indian People*) wrote:

> The Age begins with the repulse of the Arab invasions on the mainland of India in the beginning of the eighth century and ends with the fateful year AD 997 when Afghanistan passed into the hands of the Turks.
>
> With this Age, ancient India came to an end. At the turn of its last century, Sabuktigin and Mahmud came to power in Gazni. Their lust, which found expression in the following decades, was to shake the very foundations of life in India, releasing new forces. They gave birth to medieval India. Till the rise of the Hindu power in the eighteenth century, India was to *pass through a period of collective resistance.*[7] [emphasis mine]

What K.M. Munshi wrote for the series edited by R.C. Majumdar, who too held identical views, is not very different from the dominant approach characterizing Indian history writing generally. In the context of Indian nationalist historiography, the ancestry of the assumptions separating the Hindu period from the Muslim period can be firmly dated to mid-nineteenth century enterprises of writing the history of the country. It has been shown:

> This history, now, is periodized according to the distinct character of rule, and this character, in turn, is determined by the religion of the rulers. The identification here of country (*deś*) and realm (*rājatva*) is permanent and indivisible. This means that although there may be at times several kingdoms and kings, there is in truth always only one realm which is coextensive with the country and which is symbolized by the capital or the throne. The *rājatva,* in other words, constitutes the generic sovereignty of the country, whereas the capital or the throne represents the centre of sovereign statehood. Since the country is *Bhāratavarṣa,* there can be only one true sovereignty which is co-extensive with it.[8]

Historiographically, what strikes one as critical is that the 'otherness' of sovereign, medieval, Muslim India is a persistent image, and an undifferentiated, ancient, Hindu India continues to be presented as facing, first a threat and then collapse, politically and culturally, when the Muslims

[7] R.C. Majumdar, ed., *The Age of Imperial Kanauj* (vol. 4 of *The History and Culture of the Indian People*), Bombay, 2nd edn., 1964, p. vii.

[8] Chatterjee, 'Claims on the Past', p. 26.

arrive. This is a discourse which, despite the accent on synthesis and positive interaction between earlier and Islamic cultures in one variety of nationalist history writing, has not been examined adequately with reference to sources which bear upon the early phase of the association of Muslim communities with India. Indeed, the discourse continues to receive reinforcement even in recent, highly accomplished writings as a supportable mindset, and I would like to cite two recent pieces of writing which, I believe, would bear my point out as substantiating evidence. In one,[9] an attempt has been made to bring into sharp relief the apprehension of threat which Muslim invasions generated in Indian society. This, apparently, can be seen in the way in which the text of the *Rāmāyaṇa,* woven around the heroic deeds of its central character Rama, came to supply an idiom or 'vocabulary' for political imagination for the public mind in India between the eleventh and the fourteenth century. In the context of the historical situation of north India and the Deccan, in what is called the 'middle period', the following is thus asserted:

> In fact, after tracing the historical effectivity of the *Rāmāyaṇa* mytheme—tracing, that is, the penetration of its specific narrative into the realms of public discourse of post-epic India, in temple remains, 'political inscriptions', and those historical narratives that are available—it is possible to specify with some accuracy the particular historical circumstances under which the *Rāmāyaṇa* was *first deployed as a central organizing trope in the political imagination of India.*[10] [emphasis mine]

The central organizing trope was the *Rāmāyaṇa's* hero Rama, who represented the victorious divine against the ultimately subdued demon, and 'the tradition of invention—of inventing the king as Rama—begins in the twelfth century'. The need to invent the king as Rama is seen as relating to the perception of threat—against the ideal political and moral order of *Rāmārājya,* the Turuṣka marauders being the demons who posed the threat.

While thus the neat schema of periodization in terms of Hindu-Muslim divide is, by implication, restated, another way of representing the image of an absolute break in Indian history is by relating the discourse of power to the cultural hegemony of Islam. 'The "arrival" of Islam as a discourse of state power had introduced a "cultural fault-line" between the Muslims and the non-Muslims.'[11] The 'cultural resistance' against Islam as a 'discourse of power' throughout the medieval period in India, in this image, could take

[9] Sheldon Pollock, 'Ramayana and Political Imagination in India', *The Journal of Asian Studies*, vol. 53, no. 2, 1993, pp. 261–97.

[10] Ibid., p. 263.

[11] See the chapter (6) 'The Stale in Medieval North India and the Cultural Faultline', in *Struggle for Hegemony in India 1920-47: Culture, Community and Power*, ed. Shashi Joshi and B.S. Josh, vol. 3, 1941–7, Delhi, 1994.

the form of 'a strange kind of "silence" on the part of Hindu authors about their Muslim contemporaries'; it could also be of the form of 'thousands of individual acts of dogmatic ritual behaviour and evasion'.[12]

This historiography of periodization relates to the problem of perception and representation in the following ways. One, it constructs, for the historical past, an agenda of conscious public action, in the form of 'collective resistance' or 'cultural resistance'. Two, it also constructs collective consciousness for a particular past—a past which is confronted with a threat; it is this collective consciousness which can explain a 'central organizing trope in the political imagination of India'. Both constructions hinge on confident recovery of contemporary perceptions, not individual but cultural, in historical situations which are projected as understandable only in terms of irreconciliablc bi-polar differences and fixed identities.

The objective of the present work is to contest both these constructions. The main method in doing this will be the simple expedient of re-examining the sources; but as sources are voluminous, the method of re-examination itself should involve some consideration of the sources in their own cultural contexts. No study can exhaust all sources which may have a bearing on the problem under investigation, but since historians' own perceptions, rather than the source-by-itself, largely determine the selection and interpretation of sources used, any critique of available generalizations essentially means reading the same or same types of source-material with a measure of mistrust and with new curiosities. This in turn may lead to sources which have not been used adequately in the past.

I would thus like to make it clear that it is not my intention to gloss over the primary difference between Islam, which did become one of the discourses of power (but not the sole discourse because, then, what would be the dominant social discourse within the stratified 'Hindu' society?), and the cultural pattern (in a broad socio-religious sense) which was 'perceived' as and put into the basket called 'Hindu'. My attempt is also not to undermine actualities of conflict along lines, sometimes seen even contemporaneously, as Hindu or Muslim. But even this primary difference is one difference out of many, which is mostly presented out of context, and my objection is basically to the way in which Indian history continues to be truncated between 'Hindu' and 'Muslim', and, obliterating other types of difference, the projected difference is made to represent fundamental historical change as well.

While historians continue to subscribe to this notion of historical change perhaps by adhering to historiographical conventions and perhaps

[12] Ibid., pp. 148–9.

also by attributing their contemporary perceptions to the subjects of their investigation, the point to ask anew is: how does one construct perceptions of the past? To clarify, when we talk about interface between Islam and Indian society in, say, the period between the eighth century and the fourteenth century, are we not, in posing the problem the way we do (i.e. interface between Islam and Indian society), imposing the contradictory notions of polarity and homogeneity implicit in the formulation of the problem, upon a particular past? Further, in relating the actualities of conflict only to particularly constructed polarities, historians tend to underscore the conflict potential of a particular polarity to the exclusion of others; this is taken to further buttress the generalization about cultural characteristics, already made. Finally, once a particular polarity is historiographically argued, one tends to forget to ask: do perceptions change over time? If other things change in history, there is a further possibility that attitudes do so too; and, there is a further possibility too that attitudes do not constitute a homogeneity.

There is then no alternative to continuously revisiting the sources which, I have already mentioned, cannot be identified with any finality once for all. The deliberate, or, often, not so deliberate choice of sources by historians, leaves even what is available largely hidden from the audience of history. Sources being thus visible mostly in terms of the historian's monologue with them, it is all the more necessary then that other voices too intervene.

The Burden of Written Sources

> Literature may provide facts for social scientists, especially in the absence of other documents. But literature refracts as much as it reflects; one needs to take account of the 'specific density' of the literary medium, its 'refractive index', before we can truly use literary materials as documents. To use them in a literal straightforward fashion is to misuse them. . . . Unless we enter the realm of symbolic values that writers express through the 'facts' and 'objective entities', the facts themselves would be commonplace or misunderstood.
>
> —A.K. RAMANUJAN, 'Toward an Anthology of City Images', in *Urban India: Society, Space and Image*, ed. Richard G. Fox

The realm of symbolic values, or repertoire of perceptions that A.K. Ramanujan points to, could bear upon representations of historical situations in many ways, and several preliminary points need to be made here. One is that written sources that relate to the ruling groups of the period which is the primary focus of the work, and also from later periods, tend to convey cultural premises and practices of particular sections of society which—in the absence of a better alternative—may be called elite. This is not to say that the premises remain confined to permanently fixed sections of society because they are also the adopted premises of those who aspire for elite status; the channels for dissemination of cultural premises too were many. But the production of the written word, in a language like Sanskrit, was the work of the literate elite—the Brāhmanas, the Kāyasthas, the Jainas and comparable groups. The choice of the premises to be projected in the written text, whether the text is that of a land-grant inscription or that of a *mahākāvya,* at the historical moment when the text was prepared, was that of a literate elite who, in the process of creating the text, was drawing upon a well-established pool of conventions, motifs and symbols. His choices, therefore, cannot be used as material for construction of public consciousness, but only of dominant premises. The point about choice relates to the range of material the creator of texts uses; to select arbitrary samples on his behalf, when analysing the text, would be anachronistic, imposing the analyser's preferences on the author, and, from there, on to the society at large. We shall take up specific examples for elucidating these points later.

The second point is that written sources, perhaps more than other sources which may be used for historical reconstruction, demand that they be viewed not only diachronically but synchronically as well. An accent on the synchronic view is to ensure that the historian is aware of the available range. While the diachronic view will make it clear that such a textual genre as a *Carita,* woven around a central character, emerges from a certain point of time and therefore requires explanation in terms of the context of its origin, the synchronic view or the horizontal view will ensure that one does not miss out on the simultaneity of many patterns. The *Vikramāṅkadeva-carita* of Bilhaṇa, of which the central character was Vikramāditya Tribhuvanamalla of the later Cālukya royal family of what is now Karnataka, is an important text of the late eleventh century.[13] However, it is a text representing a particular genre; it is not a text which can be considered to represent the total range of poetic conventions, not to speak of the range of realities constituting eleventh-century Indian society. Consider, for example, *Subhāṣitaratnakoṣa,* an almost contemporary anthology of Sanskrit poems prepared in eastern India,[14] in which the concerns of the poets represented are very much removed from the courtly concerns of the *Vikramāṅkadeva-carita.* The two represent 'realities' of different kinds, although both may have been products

[13] *Vikramāṅkadeva-carita,* edited with an Introduction by G. Buhler, Bombay, 1875.

[14] D.D. Kosambi and V.V. Gokhale, *The Subhāṣitaratnakoṣa compiled by Vidyākara,* with an Introduction by D.D. Kosambi, Harvard Oriental Series, vol. 42, Cambridge, Mass., 1957; Daniel H.H. Ingalls, *An Anthology of Sanskrit Court Poetry: Vidyākara's 'Subhāṣitaratnakoṣa',* Harvard Oriental Series, vol. 44, Cambridge, Mass., 1965.

of the same literary tradition. If one were speaking of a period closer to our own times—say the period of Akbar—there would surely be a variety of written words (apart from the uncodified ones) besides the major texts in different languages, and they all are important—not because they contain authentic historical material—but because they originate in and relate to different contexts of the same period. One can thus cite *Bhānucandra-carita*, the 'biography' of a Jaina teacher,[15] which was written by Bhānucandra's disciple, placing him in close proximity to the emperor of Delhi, alongside a comparatively unknown inscription from Malwa.[16] The inscription eulogizes both a local family of merchants with Jaina leanings and a local Rajput family which fights local Muslim rulers and looks up to the Muslim emperor of Delhi for grant of landed estates. They are not necessarily complementary sources; they are independently important as texts with separate loci, which nevertheless suggest a linkage in a situation of simultaneity of many patterns.

Isolating a single high point in the structure of an individual text may not be a sound methodological device either. At least, cautious comparison with narratives within the text and with other texts is what would be expected of one making generalizations. Let me again cite a few examples. *Pṛthvīrāja-vijaya* of Jayānaka,[17] *Hammīramadamardana* of Jayasiṃhasūri,[18] *Madhurā-vijaya* of Gaṅgādevī and *Sāluvābhyudaya* of Rājanātha Diṇḍima[19] are all generally taken to have a single central focus: the narrative of military exploits against a Yavana or Turuṣka adversary. All these texts do have references to military exploits—quite often at variance with what actually happened—against a Yavana/Mleccha/Turuṣka adversary; there are, of course, many other texts created in the same period, which contain other narratives. How does one compare the narratives of the texts cited, which will be shown to have

[15] M.D. Desai, *Bhānuchandra Carita by his pupil Gaṇi Siddhichandra Upādhyāya*, Ahmedabad and Calcutta, 1941. The title page in nāgarī script calls it *Bhānuchandragaṇi-carita,* and the text itself calls it *Sri Bhānuchandragaṇi-prabhāvaka-puruṣa-carita*. Hereafter, the title *Bhānucandra-carita* will be used.

[16] Sadhu Ram, 'Two Inscriptions from Rampura', *Epigraphia India* (hereafter *EI*), vol. 36, 1965–6, Delhi, 1970, pp. 121–30.

[17] See Chandra Prabha, *Historical Mahākāvyas in Sanskrit (Eleventh to Fifteenth Century AD)*, Delhi, 1976, Chap. 4.

[18] For the contents of the play *Hammīramadamardana* see Bhogilal J. Sundesara, *Literary Circle of Mahāmātya Vastupāla and its Contribution to Sanskrit Literature*, Bombay, 1953, pp. 122–5.

[19] For *Madhurāvijaya* and *Sāluvābhyudaya,* see Prabha, *Historical Mahākāvyas in Sanskrit,* Chaps. 10 and 11.

different foci,[20] with narratives in such texts as Sandhyākaranandi's *Rāma-carita*[21] or Padmagupta's *Navasāhasāṅka-carita*?[22] In analysing what historians tend to take as a political narrative with a single focus but what may have had a broader significance for the creator of a text writing in a particular historical period, it is necessary to be careful about stocktaking. In other words, if one is considering adversaries in a political narrative, then it needs to be noted who, according to the author of the text, needed to be subdued by the central character of the text; isolating one opponent from a multitude of others, or one text from contemporary others, can be very much misleading when one is trying to comprehend the ideological world of the authors.

Understanding the ideological world through texts takes us on to the internal structures of the texts: both to the ways the segments of the text may be seen to have related to one another and to the ways the authors deal with conventions, language, similes, images and so on. I would like to argue that instead of being necessarily jolted into projecting a world of sharply bipolarized and antagonistic elements, the creators of texts rather tended to expand this world by using existing literary conventions to incorporate within it new empirical elements of history. These literary conventions, with their elements of diversity, also had space for perceptions of 'others' and of the threats which the society may have been perceived to have confronted. If new historical situations were perceived in terms of threats or in terms of 'others' being associated with them, the existing conventions could be extended for textual explications of the situation. This could be done, even when remaining fully cognizant of the details of a historical situation which could be stylized. Only, what was accommodated within available concepts, conventions and vocabularies, can hardly be taken as a statement made for the communication of historical reality.

[20] One can refer to *Hammīramadamardana* the importance of which is underlined in view of its being 'a drama on a contemporary historical event'. The play which, according to its author, contained all nine sentiments, is on the curbing of the pride of Hammīra, the Muslim ruler, by Vāghela ruler Vīradhavala's minister Vastupāla. But Yādava ruler Siṃhaṇa and the ruler of Lāṭa are shown to be equally troublesome adversaries in the play. Vastupāla's diplomatic manouverings against the Muslim ruler are rather complex, and include sending a false report to the Caliph of Baghdad and holding out promises to Gurjara princes with lands of the Turuṣkas; the curbing of Hammīra's pride in the end consists in entering a friendly alliance, through a kind of blackmail; B.J. Sandesara, *Literary Circle of Mahāmātya Vastupāla and its Contribution to Sanskrit Literature*, Bombay, 1953.

[21] *Rāmacarita,* ed. R.C. Majumdar, R.G. Basak and N.G. Banerji, Rajshahi, 1939.

[22] Prabha, *Historical Mahākāvyas in Sanskrit*, Chap. I.

From the foregoing, how should one characterize the written sources that bear upon the question of 'otherness' of communities that interacted with society in India from around the seventh-eighth centuries onward? I think it is indeed necessary, when one is using a cluster of texts for understanding perceptions and representations, to clarify whether our concern about perceptions was the concern of the texts at all. This is not to say that the historian's concern is invalidated that way. Nevertheless, my preliminary answer to this query would be that neither the epigraphic nor the literary texts of the early medieval period—taken in their collectivity—were composed with the purpose of communicating perceptions of communities. They had altogether different functions. The inscriptions, despite the fact that early medieval inscriptions differed substantially from their earlier counterparts in contents and in style, had one central concern: recording of gift and of patronage. The context of the gift introduced the royal element whose presence and whose temporal qualities, like the spiritual qualities of a brāhmaṇa, a perceptor or a priest, had to be located in the context of the gift. The inscriptions, even when rulers were eulogized by highlighting their real or imagined military exploits and personal qualities, were thus not political inscriptions per se, because political could not be separated from the broad social context in which grants were made. The more appropriate perspective from which to view the inscriptions would, therefore, be legitimational rather than overtly political. It is important to note this difference, because, as I shall try to demonstrate later on, legitimation, rather than any handy political explanation, will clarify in a much better way how the rulers in general—and not necessarily rulers belonging to any particular community—continued to be portrayed in the texts in 'indigenous' languages. If there are political references to other communities—and there often are in early medieval/ medieval sources—then they, I feel, have to be understood in terms of the overall context of legitimation, in which gift and patronage were what were relevant. This was a context which could—and did—make bipolar distinction, but this would be a distinction between those who could be legitimized and those who could not; this is not the distinction, as envisaged by modern scholars, between 'indigenous' and 'non-indigenous' categories.

The texts of the genre of *Carita* or *Mahākāvya* similarly were not 'historical narratives' as such; they were both 'biographies' and 'not biographies'. They were biographies in the sense that the text was woven around a historical character; they were not biographies as they were not simply intended to record only the actual events in the life of the hero, irrespective of whether the hero was a royal figure or a merchant. The portrayed life was the reflection of an ideal reality which, of course, had to match the specific station of the hero. For a king, the reality had to relate to the relevant spheres of conquests, love and munificence; for a merchant, it was the qualities of piety and munificence in consonance with social and economic status. Varieties of reference, including reference to social and ethnic groups, would constitute the world of the hero of the biography. The meaning of a particular reference, whether it relates to conquest, love, piety or munificence, should derive from the meaning of the total world—political, economic, social, cultural-ideological—of the biography; it should not stand in isolation from the meaning of the rest of the biography.[23]

It is possible to try and reconstruct perceptions and representations of 'others' from such texts, but, then, the reconstruction has to be in consonance with the overall structure of the text and its repertoire of words, expressions and images. My attempt, therefore, is not to single out but to understand multiplicity. Growing intensity of specific terms or of specific images may indeed be a pointer to historical change and change in perception. That such change is already evident in the period under discussion is not a given historical truth, necessarily not even a satisfactory assumption. The contexts in which the terms and images appear will be taken up in the next two chapters.

[23] The conventions applied to the creation of epigraphic texts as much as to those of *Caritas*. It has been recently shown that since women were not supposed to be rulers, the representations of the achievements and of the person of Kākatīya queen Rudrāmmā were those of a male ruler. However, 'The ideal of kingship was so strongly correlated with the notion of manliness that even inscriptions referring to Rudrāmādevi as a woman could praise her only in distinctly masculine ways. That is Rudrāmā's greatness as a ruler could be expressed only by lauding her heroic acts.' Further, 'Depiction of men as champions or as warriors whose fierceness struck terror in the hearts of enemies were widespread in this period. Indeed, it would appear from a survey of male *praśastis* that the main claim to legitimacy and prestige was success in battle. . . . Religious beneficence was considered *desirable* in a man but not *essential* to his fame.' Cynthia Talbot, 'Rudrama Devi, the Female King: Gender and Political Authority in Medieval India', in *Syllables of Sky: Studies in South Indian Civilization in Honour of Veleheru Naravana Rao*, ed. David Shulman, Delhi, 1995, pp. 402–3.

CHAPTER 2

Images of Raiders and Rulers

It is already well known—but apparently needs to be reiterated—that written sources from about the eighth century do not use terms which are today used as generic terms to refer to the Muslims.[1] It is not altogether true, as seems to be suggested by some, that sources reveal lack of familiarity with specifics as regards terms and concepts associated with Islam.[2] At least in the middle of the thirteenth century, there is clear evidence of familiarity with the term *Musalamāna* (literally, 'one who submits to Allah'), and of concepts which relate to the practice of Islam.[3] But such evidence is extremely rare, whereas generic terms which were in use in earlier times to denote outsiders or others to the society, were grafted on to newcomers, without even partial modifications. The general absence of a term in written sources cannot by itself be a proof that it was unfamiliar. On the other hand, it may be interesting to speculate why, if a term was known, as *Musalamāna* was known in the thirteenth century, it was not used commonly. The use as well as non-

[1] Romila Thapar, 'Imagined Religious Communities? Ancient History and the Modern Search for a Hindu Identity', in *Interpreting Early India*, ed. R. Thapar, Delhi, 1992, pp. 60–88; Anwar Hussain, 'The "Foreigners" and the Indian Society (Early Eighth Century to Thirteenth Century): A Study of Epigraphic Evidence from Northern and Western India', M.Phil. dissertation, Centre for Historical Studies, Jawaharlal Nehru University, 1993.

[2] Shashi Joshi and B.S. Josh, op. cit., p. 190.

[3] See D.C. Sircar, 'Veraval Inscription of Chaulukya-Vāghela Arjuna, 1264 AD', *EI*, vol. 34, 1961–2; Delhi, 1963, pp. 141–50; idem, *Select Inscriptions Hearing on Indian History and Civilization*, vol. 2, Delhi, 1983, pp. 402–8. The inscription was originally edited by E. Hultzsch, 'A Grant of Arjunadeva of Gujarat, Dated 1264 AD', *The Indian Antiquary* (hereafter *IA*), vol. 11, 1882, pp. 241–5.

use of particular words, in addition of course to ways they were used, may indeed be indicative of attitudes.

What were then the terms used commonly? And, do appropriate references, arranged in a chronological order, suggest any evolutionary pattern? Appendix I provides a bird's eye-view of the pattern; for the present, a general point may be made. It can be noticed, when one wades through a substantial series of comparable epigraphic records, that terms found in these records (and literary texts as well) may be broadly grouped into four categories, the classification being based on how these terms were derived. I would consider the category of ethnic names as most important, as the majority of terms used—and most regularly—derive from tribal / community names. Ethnic names are, in general, specific references, not liable to inappropriate attribution, and included in this category in their specific contexts are: Tājika, Turuṣka, Gaurī, Mudgala, Turuti (Turbati), Paṭhāṇa.

Terms derived from country of origin are Pārasīka and Garjaṇa/ Garjaṇaka. As one shall presently see, Pārasīka was originally distinctly pre-Islamic, and changed its connotation to move over to the category of generic terms, qualified to be used interchangeably with other generic terms. Garjaṇa / Garjaṇaka was derived from the placename Gazni, and referred to the ruler of Delhi. *Hammīra,* another term in common use, was derived from *āmir* and, unlike *Suratrāṇa,* which, having been derived from Sultan remained an honorific, could be a generic term, as suggested by the title of the play *Hammīramadamardana* and many references in the inscriptions. The other generic terms were: Yavana, Mleccha and Śaka.[4] All these terms were in use in early historical times; but although Yavana and Mleccha were already generic terms with reference to 'outsiders' in the early historical context, the ethnic term Śaka came to acquire, or so it appears, a generic connotation only in early medieval times, perhaps through its continued association with the Śaka era.[5]Another instance of an ethnic term changing into a generic term in the early medieval period is Turuṣka*;* its use was too frequent to have been restricted to a single ethnic connotation alone.

This, admittedly, is a brief introduction to the range of terms used and to what they seem to have conveyed; what is required now is to make more detailed reference to their contextual occurrences.

[4] See Aloka Parashar, *Mlecchas in Early India: A Study in Attitude towards Outsiders upto AD 600*, New Delhi, 1991; HP. Ray, 'The Yavana Presence in Ancient India', *Journal of the Economic and Social History of the Orient*, vol. 31, 1988, pp. 311–25.

[5] See D.C. Sircar, *Indian Epigraphy*, Delhi, 1965, pp. 258–66.

II

Two terms in early use were Pārasīka and Tājika. Pārasīka was definitely connected with pre-Islamic Persia, and for its early use, D.R. Bhandarkar's comments appear to be still pertinent:

> a Pārasīka is distinguished from a Pahlava in ancient Indian works and records. The latter is identical with Iranian Pahlav and is taken to denote a Parthian. Pārasīka, on the other hand, is the Pahlavi Parsik, denoting an inhabitant of Pars, the ancient Persis or modern Fars. It should further be remembered that the meaning which attaches to the word depends upon the period to which any particular reference to it belongs.[6]

Bhandarkar's precise identification of Pārasīkas of AD 300–700 with 'Iranians of the time of or connected with the Sassanian dynasty', and of a later period, with the 'Muhammadan inhabitants of Persia' may not apply uniformly to all Pārasīka references so neatly, but a shift in the connotation did definitely take place, making it a generic term interchangeable with Śaka, Mleccha or Yavana, rather than with a fixed connotation in relation to 'Muhammadan inhabitants of Persia'.[7] Pārasīka, in fact, can be used to question fixed relation between ethnicity and the connotation of a term. In the *Raghuvaṃśam* (iv) of Kālidāsa, king Raghu encountered the Pārasīkas, who were westerners (*pāścātya*), in his *digvijaya* undertaken on the land route. Kālidāsa tells us that Raghu

> could not bear the flush caused by wine in the lotus faces of the Yavana women; that a fierce battle took place between him and the westerners who had cavalry for their army; that he covered the earth with their bearded heads, severed by his arrows, that the survivors put off their helmets and sought his protection, and that his soldiers beguiled the fatigue of conquest with wine in vineyards covered with choicest skins.[8]

Other practices associated with the Pārasīkas are condemned in *Dharmaśāstra* texts and other genres of literature, *Vṛddha Yājñavalkya* duly dictating that on 'touching Candalas, Mlecchas, Bhillas, Pārasīkas and others and those that were guilty of the mortal sins, one should bathe together with the clothes worn'.[9] However, the references to the Pārasīkas in epigraphs and

[6] D.R. Bhandarkar, 'Pārasīka Dominion in Ancient India', *Annuls of the Bhandarkar Oriental Research Institute,* vol. 8, 1926–7, pp. 133–41.

[7] The term *Pārasīka* came to be used for Indian Muslims as well. See Vilasa grant from Andhra cited later.

[8] Bhandarkar, 'Pārasīka Dominion'.

[9] P.V Kane, 'The Pahlavas and Pārasīka in Ancient Sanskrit Literature', in *Dr. Modi Memorial Volume,* ed. Dr Modi Memorial Volume Editorial Board, Bombay, 1930, pp. 352–7.

literature from the close of the seventh century were in all likelihood to Persian settlements on the western coast and such references are devoid of any ethnic attributes. It is not at all clear when Pārasīka came to denote a Muslim; possibly, by the close of the eleventh century, when Kulottuṅga Cola claimed to have 'scattered [his] enemies [and] whose fame is spontaneously sung on the further shore of the ocean by the young women of the Persians (*Pārasi*)',[10] the term had acquired a new connotation.

The earliest occurrence of the term Tājika is in the Kavi plate from Broach (Bharoch) district, Gujarat. Dated 22 June 736, the plate[11] which records a gift of land to God Asramadeva, mentions the Tājikas in order to highlight the military achievements of Jayabhaṭa IV, Gurjara feudatory of the contemporary Maitraka ruler of Valabhi, the actual raid having been undertaken at the city of the lord of Valabhi from Sind. The context of the grant is not military, but it is intended to convey the impression that by forcibly vanquishing the Tājikas, Jayabhaṭa was able, 'even as a cloud extinguishes with its showers the fire that troubles all people', to put an end to the unending misery of the people (*aśeṣa-loka-santāpa*).

The term Tājika, it has been suggested,[12] was derived from Pahlavi Tāzīg, in turn derived from the name of the Arab tribe Tayy. However, a recent intensive probe into the various possibilities regarding the derivation of the term shows that it derived from Arabic tribal or tribal confederation of the Tayy', and, further, that 'an old Parthian formation of the name which by the third century must have been Tāzīg may be envisaged'.[13] In any case the term in use in India was thus of West Asian origin, but it was indigenized, as were other terms of the categories listed earlier. The term, in a similar

[10] E. Hultzsch, 'Four Inscriptions of Kulottuṅga Chola', *EI*, vol. 5, Delhi; repr. 1984, p. 104.

[11] V.V. Mirashi, *Inscriptions of the Kalachuri-Chedi Era*, pt. I (Corpus Inscriptionum Indicarum, vol. 4, Ootacamund, 1955, pp. 96–102. The relevant passage in the inscription reads: *Asidhārājalena Śamitaḥ prāsabham Valahhipateḥ pure yenāśeṣa-loka-santāpa—kalāpades—Tajik—ānalo Jayabhaṭajaladah eṣaḥ*. The same passage occurs, as a part of the long genealogical portion, in the Prince of Wales Museum Plates of Jayabhaṭa IV: AD 736 (lines 31–2); ibid., p. 106.

[12] D. Pingree, 'Sanskrit Evidence for the Presence of Arabs, Jews and Persians in Western India: CA 700-1300', *Journal of the Oriental Institute*, vol. 31, no. 2, 1981–2, pp. 172–82.

[13] W. Sundermann, 'An Early Attestation of the Name of the Tajiks', in *Medioiranica* [Proceedings of the International Colloquium organized by the Katholieke Universiteit Leuven from 21 to 23 May 1990 (Leuven, 1990)], ed. W. Skalmowski and A.V. Tongerloo, pp. 163–71. I am thankful to Mr Ingo Strauch of Humboldt University, Berlin, for not only giving me this reference but also making a photocopy of the article available for my use.

context, occurs in another near contemporary record from Navasari, also in Gujarat.[14] The feudatory who this time inflicted what is represented as a major defeat on the advancing Tājika army was Cālukya Pulakeśirāja. His overlord, the illustrious king Vallabha, rewarded the unique display of the feudatory's valour with such titles as *Dakṣiṇāpatha-sādhāra* (the pillar of *Dakṣiṇāpatha*), *Calukki-kul-ālaṁkāra* (ornament of the family of the Calukkis), *Pṛthivī-Vallabha* (beloved of the earth) and *Amvartaka-nivartayitṛ* (repeller of the unrepellable). Dated 21 October 739, the Navasari plates of Pulakeśirāja provide a graphic description of the devastations caused by the Tājika army which had set out to cause more devastations:

> When the army of the Tājikas,—which poured forth arrows, javelins and iron-headed clubs; which destroyed, with its rapidly brandished and glittering swords, the prosperous Saindhava, Kacchella, Saurāṣṭra, Cāvoṭaka, Maurya, Gurjara and other kings; which, desiring to enter Dakṣiṇāpatha . . . with a view to vanquish all Southern kings, came, in the very first place, to conquer the *viṣaya* of Navasārika, which rendered the regions between the quarters dusky with the dust of the ground raised by the hard and noisy hoofs of its galloping horses; the bodies (of warriors) in which appeared dreadful as their armours, were reddened by very large streams of blood (gushing) from the intestines which came out of the cavities of their big bellies, as they impetuously rushed forth and were completely pierced by spear-heads; which had previously not been vanquished even by numerous eminent chiefs among hosts of kings, who offered their heads in return for high honour and gifts they had received from their lord; who opposed it, biting mercilessly both their lips with the tips of their teeth; who, though they were great warriors and had their sharp swords reddened by the mass of blood that flowed when the sides of their loins and trunks of hostile elephants were rent on several extensive battlefields, could not attain success; who cut off the necks of their enemies' heads, as if they were plucking the stalks of lotuses, hitting them with their horse-shoe-shaped sharp arrows which were quickly discharged for the destruction of their adversaries; whose bodies were covered with a coat of bristling hair on account of their martial spirit and excitement,— was defeated in the forefront of the battle in which headless trunks began a circular dance to the accompaniment of the loud noise of drums beaten continuously in joy caused, as it were, by the thought: 'Today at least we have, by laying down our heads, paid off the debt we owed to our lord in (this) one life.'

This extensive, involved passage, offering a gory description of the battle between Avanijanāśraya Pulakeśirāja and his loyal retainers on one side and the Tājikas on the other, is cited here as an appropriate text for the study of representation. The passage represents an actual battle fought, but uses various literary conventions to take the description beyond ordinary

[14] Mirashi, *Inscriptions of the Kalachuri-Chedi Era*, pt. 1, pp. 137–45.

portrayal in order to project the loyal achievements of a feudatory, the loyalty of whose own subordinates contributes in making the imagery of the battle and the battlefield so vividly splashed with colour. The evidence of the Navasari plates is commonly cited to highlight successful national resistance in the face of threat to the integrity of the country,[15] but while analysing the evidence as bearing upon a historical event, it is necessary to remember that a description of this kind is rather unique, and, therefore, needs to be juxtaposed with other references to Tājika and other raids, and, second, that according to the evidence of the plates, the text was written by 'illustrious Bappabhaṭṭi, the *Mahāsāndhi-vigrahika* and *Sāmanta,* who has attained the *Pañcamahāśabda* and is the son of the *Mahābalādhikṛta* Haragaṇa'. The ancestry and the station of the author would surely have reflected on the vividness of the imagery.

The two inscriptions from Gujarat, almost contemporary but differing considerably in their statements about the achievements of Jayabhaṭa IV and Pulakeśirāja, focus on their respective victories over the Tājikas in contrast to the achievements of their ancestors in the genealogical tables. However, the way the Tājikas and others are mentioned in records elsewhere and in subsequent periods need also to be noted; this will have a bearing on how we understand the contextual meaning of a particular reference in a totality of statements.

The point may perhaps be effectively stated by analysing another early, eighth-century inscription, referring to the Tājikas. The inscription of Pratīhāra Vatsarāja, dated AD 795, and of uncertain provenance,[16] was intended to record the construction of a temple of Caṇḍikā by a member of a subordinate family of the Pratīhāras. The record refers to the Pratīhāra rulers Nāgabhaṭa I and Vatsarāja, and attributes sovereign kingship (*sārvabhauma-nṛpatitva*) to Vatsarāja achieved through victories over Karṇāṭa and Lāṭa in the south, which took his armies down to the southern ocean, his victory

[15] See, for example, the comments on the Arab raids of the period: 'Either Śīluka or his successor was on the throne when the Arabs swept over the whole Rājputānā and Gujarāt, and advanced as far as Ujjayinī. The Gurjara kingdom of Jodhpur was overrun, but the Pratīhāra king Nāgabhaṭa of Avantī withstood this terrible shock and hurled back the invaders. The credit of saving western India from the hands of the Arab invaders belongs to him, and he shares the glory with the Chalukya king Avanijanāśraya Pulakeśirāja who stopped their advance into southern India.

'The Arab invasion must have brought about great changes in the political condition in western India by destroying or weakening numerous small states.' R.C. Majumdar, *The Classical Age* (vol. 3 of *The History and Culture of the Indian People*), Bombay, 4th edn., 1988, p. 155.

[16] K.V. Ramesh and S.P. Tewari, 'An Inscription of Pratīhāra Vatsarāja. Śaka 717', *EI*, vol. 41, Delhi, 1989, pp. 49–57.

over Jayāpīḍa, which took his army to the Himalayan heights, his victory over the Lord of Gauḍa, as also by virtue of his victories over Mleccha and Kīra kings, respectively of the western and northern quarters. Vatsarāja's subordinate Śrīvarmaka too claimed several victories, including one on the Tājika ruler who was taken captive (*baddhahṛrta-sakala-jagajjāgaras-Tajikeśo*). Others defeated by him were: Keśari, who was forced to pay tribute; the ruler of hill tribes who were punished, and Vyāghra, the powerful Tomara king. Victories over enemies of Karṇāṭa and Gauḍa are claimed by feudatory Śrīvarmaka's son Gallaka as well in the record.

As can be seen from another record, also mentioning the Tājikas and belonging to the Rāṣṭrakūṭas of the Deccan, the terms of representation of victories achieved over enemies are in accordance with the convention which seeks to place the ruler, sometimes through the mediation of his subordinates, in a position of universal sovereignty.[17] The convention underlines the need for multiplicity of enemies who are vanquished; further, acknowledgement of defeat is opposed to the concerns of sovereignty. If at all defeat has to be acknowledged, it has to be couched in terms acceptable to the convention. The Rāṣṭrakūṭa grant, that of Kṛṣṇa III (939–67) from Chinchani in Thane and datable to the middle of the tenth century,[18] credits the ruler with victories over Pāṇḍya, Oḍra, Siṃhala, Cola, Pārasīka, Andhra, Draviḍa, Barbara, Tājika, Vaṃkina, Hūṇa, Khasa, Gurjjara and Mālavīyaka. The list is impressive, as was the projected status of the Rāṣṭrakūṭas in their records, and the fact that the Tājikas and the Pārasīkas should be mentioned among those who were subdued by Kṛṣṇa III is additionally significant. The Pārasīkas were in all probability an important community of western India located within Rāṣṭrakūṭa territories; some representatives of the Tājikas were political subordinates of the Rāṣṭrakūṭas in western India. In fact, another Chinchani grant of an earlier date, of AD 926, belonging to the period of Rāṣṭrakūṭa Indra III, refers to Madhumatī of the Tājika community who had received the entire *maṇḍala* of Saṃyāna, on western coast, from Kṛṣṇaraja II (878–915).[19] Madhumatī, obviously a Sanskritized form of Muhammad, was the son of Sāhiyarahāra (or Yarahāra), and he had another name Sugatipa. As a feudatory ruler of *Saṃyāna maṇḍala*, appointed by the Rāṣṭrakūṭas, Sugatipa was involved in projects of a religious nature, to be referred to in the next chapter, but as a governor, his position was similar to that of a member of

[17] Apart from other qualities, the hero of a *mahākāvya* was to possess the urge for conquest. See David Smith, *Ratnākara's Haravijaya: An Introduction to the Sanskrit Court Epic*, Delhi, 1985, pp. 29–30.

[18] D.C. Sircar, 'Rashtrakuta Charters from Chinchani', *EI*, vol. 32, Delhi, repr. 1987, pp. 55–60.

[19] Ibid.

the family of Tājikas who were closely associated with the Kadambas of Candrapura and Goa. G.M. Moraes, on the basis of inscriptional evidence preserved in a later Portuguese version, suggests that this association dates to the time of Guhalladeva II (980–1005?). When Guhalladeva's pilgrimage to Somnath was interrupted, he had to make his way to Goa. 'A native of this city named Madummod, of Tāji origin, the wealthiest among all sea-faring traders, a person of great wisdom, rendered a great and public service to the above-mentioned king Guhaldev.'[20] The city of Goa which was made the capital of his kingdom by Kadamba Jayakeśi I (1050–80) 'owed a substantial part of its prosperity to the wise administration of Saḍano, a grandson of the merchant Muhammada who . . . had rendered valuable service to Guhalladeva. Jayakeśi appointed him governor of the Konkan. Prudent, just and liberal, he was well-versed in mathematics and "the fourteen arts, the four resources, and the seven solicitudes".'[21] According to sources used by Moraes, in 1053 Saḍano established in the capital a charitable institution which arranged food for the poor and the helpless and lodgings for the pilgrims; the resources for running the institution came from trading vessels and merchants from foreign countries.

Saḍano, the competent administrator, is obviously identical with Sadhana mentioned in the Panjim plates of Jayakeśi I, dated AD 1059. The inscription has the following details about the family, described as of Tājika descent:

> There was one Āliyama, the peaceful, who was born in the city of Śrīvaimūlya. He was of Tājiya descent. He was intelligent and derived his wealth from the possession of ships. His son Madhumada was, like full moon, delight to the eyes of the people. To Madhumada was born Sadhana who was strong; he became equal of Keśirāja (Jayakeśi) in the matter of protecting the realm. His munificence removed the misery of the distressed and his strength put an end to his enemies. The good conduct of that wise man attracted the minds of the honest persons.[22]

The Tājika presence in western India was on a scale which may be considered not too insignificant for the formation of images about them; they would be considered as Mlecchas, despite the deliberate Sanskritization of their ethnic and personal names, and the reference to the Mlecchas and the Tājikas in the inscription of 795, of Pratīhāra Vatsarāja, need not be taken to relate to two separate communities. In fact, both Yavana and Mleccha were terms which, after having acquired a generic connotation suitable for application to outsiders, continued in use. The mention of the Yavanas in

[20] G.M. Moraes, *The Kadamba Kula: A History of Ancient and Medieval Karnataka*, Bombay, 1931, pp. 171–2.

[21] Ibid., pp. 185–6.

[22] Panaji Copperplates of Jayakeśi I of AD 1059 in ibid., Appendix 3, no. 2.

the Kharepatan (Ratnagiri district, Maharashtra) inscription of 1095[23] of the time of Śilāhāra ruler Anantadeva and of the Mlecchas in the Vadavali grant (Thane, Maharashtra) of 1127[24] of the time of Śilāhāra Aparāditya I would have related to the Tājikas who, as already pointed out, had a significant political presence in western India in early medieval times, to the extent of being listed among adversaries even when they could be appointed as governors and could be seen as contributors to the promotion of an ideal socio-religious order.

To return to the question of representation in terms of literary convention, it may be instructive to study the images which are projected about the Tājikas in the specific context of western India of early medieval times. Tājika raiders of the Navasari record of AD 739 were obviously considered capable of causing political devastations; the Yavanas of the Kharepatan plate, who overran the Konkan country as a result of a civil war after Mummuni, harassed the Gods and brāhmaṇas (*devadvijāti-pramatha-vidhi*) and were 'violent and vile' (*ugra, pāparāśi*). These are traits which may be seen as conforming to what the Yavanas or Mlecchas would generally be associated with. However, the general is not necessarily universal, and what the Chinchani plates tell us about the activities of the Arab governor Sugatipa will, again, have to be understood, and in a specific context, of what is associable with the Tājikas/Yavanas/Mlecchas. The point about the general and the specific may also be explored by trying to see the relationship between the Tājikas/Mlecchas and the norms of the existing social order. Note, for example, the case of Chittukka, who according to the Vadavali plates (Thane, Maharashtra) of Śilāhāra Aparāditya I (AD 1127), was an *asura*—a demon—born to devastate the world (*jagad-dalayitum*).[25] 'All the feudatories gathered round him . . . the wealth of religious merit was destroyed, the elders perished, refugees were harassed, all townsmen and their servants were ruined and all prosperity of the kingdom came to an end.[26] The calamity to the Śilāhāra kingdom, seen in general terms of devastation to the world, was caused by an individual who, when Aparāditya fought him single-handed, with only one horse, ran away and sought refuge

[23] V.V. Mirashi, *Inscriptions of the Śilāhāras* (Corpus Inscriptionum Indicarum, vol. 6), Delhi, 1977, pp. 115–20.

[24] Ibid., pp. 120–7.

[25] Ibid., Verse 20 of the record reads:

Āsīt—k'opyasuro—jagad-dalayituṃ Chittukka-nāmāntakas-tasyaivaṃ ca samastam-eva-milataṃ sāmantacakraṃ tataḥ dhvaste dharmadhane gateṣu guruṣu kliṣṭe vibhāsaṃśraye sīrṇṇe jīrṇṇapuraprajāparijane naṣṭe ca rāṣṭrodaye.

[26] Later references to Tājikas seem to be found only in texts. See M. Monier-Williams, *A Sanskrit-English Dictionary*, Delhi; repr., 1993, p. 441.

with the Mlecchas. The inscription does associate, in the end, the Mlecchas with calamity, but not as its originator in this specific context. At the same time, as will be mentioned later, the Mlecchas are generators of calamity in other situations in which Mleccha domination causes total ruin of existing political and social order. The general tenor of how the Tājikas as Mlecchas or as Yavanas would be perceived and represented, which would sometimes accord with representations of individuals from other social groups, would pose a contradiction with other types of representation. It will have to be seen whether contemporary conventions can in any way illuminate and resolve this contradiction.

III

References to Tājikas in inscriptions appear to discontinue after the tenth century,[27] although, judging from the history of commercial and other contacts with the Arab world,[28] it is rather surprising that the term does not continue to figure with any importance in the epigraphic and other records of western India. The term which assumes increasing importance is Turuṣka, although this preliminary statement requires several qualifications. First, it is not that the term Turuṣka is of later usage than Tājika and replaces it. Second, it is not Turuṣka alone which comes to be in use. For example, the term Śaka can be seen to be in use where one could expect Turuṣka. Similarly, as can be seen from the Vilasa grant of Prolaya Nāyaka, of the first half of the fourteenth century from Andhra Pradesh,[29] Turuṣka could be

[27] See V.K. Jain, *Trade and Traders in Western India (AD 1000–1300)*, Delhi, 1900, passim.

[28] N. Venkataramanayya and M. Somasokhara Sharma, 'Vilasa Grant of Prolaya Nayaka', *EI*, vol. 32, 1957–8, Delhi; repr., 1987, pp. 239–68.

[29] P. Prasad, 'The Turushka or Turks in Late Ancient Indian Documents', *Proceedings of the Indian History Congress*, 55th Session, Aligarh, 1994; Delhi, 1995, pp. 170–5. André Wink summarizes views on the nomenclature and origin of the Turks thus: 'The very word "Turk" or "Türk" appears as the name of a Central-Asian nomad people only from the 6th century onwards, when in 552 the "Turk" Qaghanatc was founded on the Orkhon river in Mongolia. The Chinese name for the Turks was *Tu-Kueh*. which was apparently derived from *Türküt*, the Mongol plural of *Türk*. The Greeks called them *Tourkoi*, the Arabs *Atrak* (sg. *Turk*), while in new Persian they became known as *Turkan* (sg. *Turk*). Originally, *Türk* was an ethnonym which was associated with a small tribe headed by the Ashina clan: it meant "the strong one" and within the semantic range of a whole series of tribal names which connoted "force", "violence", "ferociousness", and so on'; André Wink, 'India and Central Asia: The Coming of the Turks in the Eleventh Century', in *Ritual, State and History in South Asia: Essays in Honour of J.C. Heesterman*, ed. A.W. van Den Hock. D.H.A. Kolff and M.S. Oort, Leiden, New York, Köln, 1992, p. 755. It is

substituted not only by such terms as Yavana, but by another term initially of a different ethnic origin, Pārasīka, as well.

Probably mentioned as *Tu-Kiue* in the Chinese annals of Tang and other dynasties.[30] Turuṣka is mentioned in early Indian literary sources from about the seventh century onward: in the *Harsa Carita* of Bāṇa who distinguished them from the Pārasīkas; in the *Garuḍa, Vāmana* and *Bhāgavata Purāṇas*; in *Amarakośa*; in the *Kāvya Jānakīharaṇa* of Kumāradāsa[31] and other texts. The *Rājatarangiṇi* reference to Kaṇiṣka and his successors as Turuṣka[32] is perhaps to be explained in terms of the manner in which the term Turuṣka was being used with reference to Shahiyas of Kabul, to even the Tibetans, and to the rulers of the north in general in the *Kumārapāla-carita* which specifies Caulukya Kumārapāla's conquests by relating them to the cardinal directions in which they were undertaken: Gaṅgā on the east, Vindhyas on the south, Sindhu on the west, and Turuṣka country on the north. Before, however, the actual establishment of the Turkish Sultanate in Delhi, the Turuṣkas start figuring on the political horizons of rulers located in different parts of the subcontinent. Perhaps the earliest epigraphic document to refer to the Turuṣkas as political adversaries is a fragmentary Sarada inscription from Hund (Attock, Pakistan), assigned, on palaeographic grounds, to the second half of the eighth century.[33] K.V. Ramesh finds in this document reference to the routing of a Muslim army in the Sindhu country by the local ruler Anantadeva,[34] but with reference to the evidence of Al-Beruni and Kalhaṇa regarding the Turuṣkas, it has alternatively been suggested that it was the ethnic Turks before conversion, who are mentioned in documents of this period.[35]

Whatever be the religious affiliation of the ethnic Turks of the Hund record, the Sagar Tal (Gwalior) inscription of Pratīhāra king Vatsarāja of the ninth century[36] refers to the Turuṣkas in a manner which is similar to how

---

possible that some of the Sanskrit appellations such as *atibala* used with reference to the Turuṣkas were literal translations of tribal connotations mentioned by Wink.

[30] Cited in G.R. Nandargikar, *The Raghuvanśa of Kālidāsa*, Bombay, 3rd revd. and enl. edn., 1897, pp. 123–4.

[31] *Rājatarangiṇī*, 1.170.

[32] K.V. Ramesh, 'A Fragmentary Sarada Inscription from Hund', *EI*, vol. 38, Delhi, 1971, pp. 94–8.

[33] K.V. Ramesh, *Indian Epigraphy*, vol. 1, Delhi, 1984, pp. 90–1.

[34] Prasad, 'Turushkas'.

[35] R.C. Majumdar, 'The Gwalior Prasasti of the Gurjara-Pratīhāra King Bhoja', *EI*, vol. 18, pp. 99–114; D.C. Sircar, 'Gwalior Stone Inscription of Bhoja I (*c.* 836-85 AD)', *Select Inscriptions*, vol. 2, pp. 242–6.

[36] F. Kielhorn, 'Khalimpur Plate of Dharmapaladeva', *EI*, vol. 4, Delhi; repr. 1979, pp. 243–54.

they figure in other early medieval records before the establishment of the Delhi Sultanate, i.e. by listing them among other enemies of the ruler. The extensive achievements of Pratīhāra Nāgabhaṭa II, which included victories over the countries of Andhra, Sindhu, Vidarbha and Kaliṅga, extended to the seizure of the hill forts of the kings of Ānartta, Mālava, Kirāta, Turuṣka, Vatsa and Matsya. The Yavana king,[37] of the Khalimpur plate of Pāla ruler Dharmapāla, a formidable adversary of the Pratīhāras, approved, along with kings of Bhoja, Madra, Kuru, Yadu, Avanti, Gandhāra and Kīra, the installation of the king of Kānyakubja by Dharmapāla; perhaps he too was a Turuṣka, and his inclusion, among a number of rulers of northern and central India, suggests a pattern which is similar to the inclusion of the Turuṣka among a number of political adversaries.

References to Turuṣkas in a similar vein occur in many inscriptions of the period, and it is not necessary to cite them all. Translations of two verses occurring in the inscriptions of the Kalacuris of Madhya Pradesh illustrate further the point made above. It is found in the Amoda plates (Bilaspur district, Madhya Pradesh) of Pṛthvīdeva, dated AD 1079: 'By that king was erected on the earth a pillar of victory after forcibly dispossessing the kings of Kośala and Vaṅga, ruler of Koṅkaṇa, the lord of Śākambharī, the Turuṣka, the descendant of Raghu, of their treasure, horses and elephants'.[38]

Another verse, occurring in the Jabalpur inscription of 1167 of Kalacuri Jayasiṃha[39] and repeated in the Kumbhi plates (1180–1)[40] and the Umariya plates (1192–3) of his son Vijayasiṃha,[41] refers to the military might of Jayasiṃha: 'On hearing of his coronation, the Gurjara king disappeared, the Turuṣka lost the strength of his arms, the lord of Kuntala renounced all love sports, and other kings also, leaving the earth through apprehension, crossed the ocean.'

The Turuṣka was thus not the only foe, and even the unparalleled valour of Vāghela Lavaṇaprasāda, crushing the Turuṣka king 'who had spattered the earth with the blood flowing from the cut-off heads of numerous kings' does not refer to the Turuṣka as his single adversary.[42] The epigraphic document of 1253, referring to it, also mentions Lavaṇaprasāda's victories over Raṇasiṃha who resembled Rāvaṇa, over the Cāhamāna king of Nadol, the Paramāra king of Dhar, and the kings of the Deccan and of Maru.

[37] V.V. Mirashi, *Inscriptions of the Kalachuri-Chedi Era*, pt. 2, pp. 402, 404–5.

[38] Ibid., pt. I, pp. 324–31.

[39] Ibid., pt. 2, p. 649.

[40] U. Jain, 'Umariya Plates of Vijayasiṃhadeva', *EI*, vol. 41, 1975–6, Delhi, 1989, pp. 38–48.

[41] G. Bühler, 'An inscription from Dabhoi', *EI*, vol. 1, Delhi; repr. 1983, pp. 20–32.

Epigraphic documents of the period, taken collectively, are in fact replete with references to who could be perceived as political adversaries and to the metaphors of heroes: they point, not to singularity, but to multiplicity.

IV

Sanskrit texts, which style themselves as *Mahākāvyas,* often refer to the Yavanas, Mlecchas, Turuṣkas interchangeably, and they too do not carry the impression of the emergence of a single foe, as a literary motif, posing threat to the military might of the central character of the *Mahākāvya.* One can assume that, from the point of view of the literary idiom, this would not have been desirable and in consonance with the intended status of the hero. A detailed examination of the texts from this perspective cannot be a part of the present study, but the point can be made by using one general study on Sanskrit 'Historical' *Mahākāvyas*[42] and by referring to at least one medieval *Mahākāvya*[43] in some detail.

Pṛthvīrāja-vijaya of Jayānaka,[44] one of the early texts of the genre of historical *Mahākāvya,* centres around Cāhamāna Pṛthvīrāja who, as a hero, is characterized as *dhīrodātta,* and who, inexplicably, continues to be designated by modern historians as 'the last Hindu emperor of India'. Written possibly between 1191 and 1193, *Pṛthvīrāja-vijaya* begins with an account of the ancestry of Pṛthvīrāja, tracing his lineage to the Sun, and the narrative moves through generations of Cāhamāna rulers till it reaches Pṛthvīrāja. Among Pṛthvīrāja's predecessors, Ajayarāja and Arṇorāja are shown as having encountered and defeated the Muslims, and, of course, *Pṛthvīrājavijaya* is about Pṛthvīrāja's own victory over the Muslims. But in terms of his priority, when Pṛthvīrāja attained maturity to rule the kingdom, first was his campaign against Nāgārjuna, who had taken possession of Guḍapura. Pṛthvīrāja also resolved to vanquish beef-eating Mleccha Gaurī (i.e. Ghuri), and bestowed gifts on a messenger who brought news from Gujarat of the routing of Gaurī (Ghuri) army; but then the narrative, in the penultimate canto of the text, moves off in a different direction: Pṛthvīrāja retires to a picture gallery and becomes absorbed in a painting portraying the beauty of Tilottamā.

[42] Chandra Prabha, *Historical Mahākāvyas in Sanskrit (Eleventh to Fifteenth Century* AD*),* Delhi, 1970.

[43] *Rāṣṭrauḍhavaṃśamahākāvyam,* published as Embar Krishnamacharya, ed., *Rāṣhṭrauḍhavaṃśa Kāvya of Rudrakavi,* with an introduction by C.D. Dalal, Gaekwad's Oriental Series, No. 5, Baroda, 1917.

[44] See the summary of the contents in Prabha, *Historical Mahākāvyas,* Chap. 4.

Pṛthvīrāja-vijaya, in the form in which it is available now, is an incomplete text, and one is thus deprived of the text's detail of Pṛthvīrāja's victory over and representation of Gaurī in the last canto of the text. However, another text, *Hammīra-mahākāvya,*[45] written perhaps in the second half of the fifteenth century, around another Cāhamāna ruler Hammīra of Raṇastambhapura, also has many references to conflicts with the Turuṣkas, interspersed with references to conflicts and intrigues with other kings. To Simharaja, a predecessor of Hammīra, is attributed a victory over Hetima, a Mleccha general; but Siṃharāja's *digvijaya* (conquest of all quarters) is directed against Karṇāṭa, Lāṭa, Cola, Gurjara and Aṅga. In *Hammīra-mahākāvya's* continuous narration of events, of the period between the death of Pṛthvīrāja IV and Hammīra, conflict with the Mlecchas is a recurrent theme; but here too references to such conflicts are combined with references to conflicts with other kingdoms, court intrigues, and religious benefactions and other activities. The motif of *digvijaya* is also used for Hammīra (whose name as that of his brother Suratrāṇa are derived respectively from *āmir* and *sultān*) and covered, as mentioned in the text, Bhīmarasapura, Gaḍhamaṇḍala, Dhāra, Ujjayinī, Medāpaṭa and Acaleśvara. Hammīra's relation with Alauddin, Sultan of Delhi, is represented as one of high intrigues. Hammīra insults his own official; the official seeks refuge at the court of Delhi; to avenge his insult, Alauddin enlists support from Anga, Telaṅga, Magadha, Mahīśura and other regions. In the final encounter with Alauddin, Hammīra, frustrated by the treachery of his subordinates, kills himself; one of the few trusted subordinates who fight for Hammīra in his last encounter is Mahimasāhi, a Yavana.

Encounters with Turuṣka or Yavana rulers of the south figure prominently in some texts written in that region. *Madhurā-vijaya,*[46] which was written by Gaṅgādevī in the second half of the fourteenth century in celebration of Vijayanagara prince Kampana's victory over the Madura Sultans, uses motifs found in other texts as well. One of several descriptions of Bukka, father of Kampana and one of the founders of Vijayanagara, is that he was born to free the world of the Mlecchas. However, when Bukka advised Kampana on his plan of campaign, Kampana's adversaries were to be Camparāya, ruler of Taṇḍiramaṇḍala and of the city of Kāñcī, and several forest kings, before he was to proceed against the Sultan of Madura. Kampana's success in the south led to the establishment of Marataka as the capital of the new province, and, the text asserts, kings from Magadha, Mālava, Sevuṇa, Siṃhala, Ḍramila, Kerala and Gauḍa waited at the gates for their turn to pay Kampana their

[45] Ibid., Chap. 9.

[46] Ibid., Chap. 10.

homage. Kampana, in the end, achieved success against the Yavanas of Madura through divine intervention.

Sāluvābhyudaya, written around 1480 by Rājanātha Diṇḍima,[47] is about another Vijayanagara figure Sāluva Narasiṃha. Sāluva Mangi, an ancestor of Narasiṃha, had, in his time, set out to defeat Mleccha *suratrāṇa* of the south and had, it is stated, removed fears of Kerala, Cola and Pāṇḍya kings. Cantos 3–13 of the text focus on the *Cakravartī* aspirations of Narasiṃha who fought against Kaliṅga, Cola and Pāṇḍya; marched down to the *setu* of Rāma, and then on to Anantaśayanam; achieved victory over Turuṣka; and then proceeded through Daśārṇa to the Himalayas. Kings of Aṅga, Koṅkaṇa, Kaliṅga, Khala, Tila, Kāruṣa, Gurjara, Lāṭa and so on acknowledged his suzerainty, and even after his anointment as a *Cakravartī* in front of God Viśveśvara of Kāśī, he went on to defeat Vaṅga, Kaliṅga, Gauḍa, Prāgjyotiṣa and a host of other countries. He also defeated the Turuṣkas, who are stated to have been endowed with various weapons and who tortured the earth.

Another interesting text, from the point of view of representation of historical events, as also that of relation with the Yavanas is *Rāṣṭrauḍhavaṃśa-mahākāvyam,* written by Rudrakavi, a poet from the south (*dakṣiṇādig-bhava-kavi*), at the instance of his patron king Nārāyaṇa Śāha, Bagula ruler of Mayūragiri, in 1596.[48] The original seat of the Rāṣṭrauḍha family is traced in the text to Kānyakubja, and it is given both solar and lunar descent through divine intervention. The narrative moves through thirty-eight generations of the family, till it reaches the time of Nārāyaṇa Śāha's son Pratāpa Śāha. Gajamalladeva, twenty-sixth in descent from the earliest member of the lineage, is stated to have defeated the Gurjaras and the Mālavas, and after having killed Alauddin (*Alāvadinam Yavanādhināthaṃ*),[49] to have taken his kingdom. His son Malugi is stated to have captured Rāmarāja of Devagiri, but at the humble request of Rāmarāja's minister Hemādri, released him, after making him a feudatory (*sāmantamādhāya punar-mumoca*).[50] Nānadeva, twenty-eighth in descent, was a casualty at the hands of crores of Turuṣka soldiers of Dillīśvara (*Koṭi-Turuṣka-sainyair*)[51] who had conquered Karṇāṭa, Lāṭa, Utkala, Cola, Gauḍa, Kaliṅga, Vaṅga and other countries. However, Khaḍgasena, Nānadeva's grandson, is stated to have defeated 8,000 Mughal warriors along with their leader Mallikā (*Sa Mallikākhyam Yavanādhinātham*

[47] Ibid., Chap. 11.

[48] E. Krishnamacharya, op. cit., Introduction. The Bagula rulers were chiefs of Baglana, between Surat and Nandurbar, in the Mughal *Suba* of Gujarat. See A.R. Khan, *Chieftains in the Mughal Empire During the Reign of Akhar*, Simla, 1977, pp. 86–7.

[49] *Rāṣṭrauḍhavaṃśa-mahākāvyam*, 2.11.

[50] Ibid., 3.13.

[51] Ibid., 3.33.

jitv-āṣṭasahasra-Mugala-vīrān).[52] Successes against the Yavanas, as also other rulers marked the times of Rāma, Nānadeva II and Bhairavasena. In fact, Bhairavasena, while he offered protection to the ruler of Maṇḍapaparvata (Mandu) by defeating one Sulema Śāha, at the same time extended help to Bāhādura Śāha, the Sultan of Gujarat (*Gurjaradeśa-pātrisāha Sulatāna Bāhādura*) who was a *Turuṣka-narendra* and was protecting his subjects with 'respectful adherence to the *dharma* appropriate to his own descent' (*nijavaṃśocita-dharma-saṃbhrameṇa*).[53] Bhairavasena's help extended to campaigns in the south, against Citrakūṭa and against the Mughal ruler Humayun (*Humāyu Mugilādhirājaḥ*). Bhairavasena was regarded as a friend (*mitra*) by the Sultan of Gujarat and was generously rewarded by the latter for his friendship.

Amicable contact with the Mughal monarchy and court began with Akabbara, a *kṣoṇipati* and *avanipurandara,* when Vīrasena, Bhairavasena's son, spent some time at the Mughal court. Although Nārāyaṇa Śāha, son of Bhairavasena and patron of the author of this *mahākāvya,* lent initial support to the Ahmednagar ruler Burahāṇa Śāha, the arrival of Akbar's son Murada Śāha in Broach, with orders for Nārāyaṇa Śāha to extend support to Murāda, made both Nārāyaṇa and his son Pratāpa to switch allegiance to the representative from Delhi.

Pratāpa Śāha, depicted in the text as a great plunderer, was on the forefront of the assault on the capital of Nijāma Śāha of Ahmednagar, and in the concluding part of the *mahākāvya,* it is claimed that Pratāpa was loved by (*praṇayi*) *Śāha Murādarājaśrīkhānakhāna-kṣitipa.*[54]

Obviously, this selective gist of the text leaves out other details of claimed military achievements, against Yavanas, and non-Yavanas, religious benefactions which interspersed with campaigns of victory, and of conventional romance and intrigue. What emerges even from this selective gist—and from the *mahākāvyas* cited above—is that war against Turuṣka/ Yavana (even when Yavanas may be depicted as allies) had by the medieval period become a part of the *digvijaya* lore, and the narrative world of the authors of the *mahākāvyas* had to be characterized by contestation for political authority by contestants of heterogeneous origin. In the *Rāṣṭrauḍhavaṃśa-mahākāvya,* the undisputed authority of course lay with Śāha Śrīmad-Akabbara (Akbar), but that was not irreconciliable, till the end, with the 'sovereign' status of *Mayūragirikeśari-Śrī-mahārājadhirāja-Śrī Nārāyaṇa Śāha.*

[52] Ibid., 3.39.

[53] Ibid., 6.11.

[54] Ibid., 20.84 and 20.87.

V

I have been trying to show, by citing epigraphic and literary sources, that as raiders and contestants for political power, the Tājikas and the Turuṣkas were depicted by contemporary authors as among many claimants in a situation of intense and constant competition. Whatever the political history of the period, even of the time of Akbar, this was what informed, through the use of literary convention, the narrative structure of the texts. The question to proceed to from this would be: How is Turuṣka rule perceived? What kind of break, if any, in the genealogy of rule, is perceived in the available documents, once the Sultanate came to be established in Delhi?

There is a cluster of interesting epigraphs of the thirteenth century from the Delhi region, which originated mostly from the merchant families of the area and to which we may turn for an initial answer to this query.

I start with the quite well-known Palam Baoli inscription of AD 1276,[55] almost the whole of which is in Sanskrit, written by Paṇḍita Yogīśvara. One notices that the inscription contains three genealogies. The genealogy of *ṭhakkura* Uḍaḍhara, a *purapati* in Śrīyoginīpura (Delhi), who had constructed numerous extensive *dharmaśālās* and was then constructing a well, to the east of Pālambagrāma (Palam) and west of Kumumbapura, for religious merit, derived from a recorded *vaṃśāvalī* which incorporated the separate genealogies of his parents. The other genealogy was that of the recent and current rulers of Delhi, starting with Sahavadina (Sihabuddin) and coming up to Śrī Hammīra Gayāsaṃdīna (Ghiyasuddin Balban). These rulers are listed as a part of a genealogy of rule. The *sāmrājya* (sovereign state corresponding to the universe) is represented as belonging to its emperor Saṅkara (Śiva) whose *abhiṣeka* was performed by the celestial river Ganga.

According to the Palam Baoli inscription, it was Lord Saṅkara who was thus the emperor of the Universe, but in the kingdom of Hariyānaka, in which Śrīyoginīpura or Ḍhillī was located, it was a succession of royal families who enjoyed the earth: first the Tomaras, followed in succession by the Cauhāṇas and then, currently, by the Śakas.[56]

[55] P. Prasad, *Sanskrit Inscriptions of Delhi Sultanate 1191–1526*, Delhi, 1990, pp. 3–15. For Palam Baoli and other Sanskrit inscriptions of the Sultanate period from Delhi and Uttar Pradesh, I have generally, though not solely, depended on this work.

[56] The Palam Baoli inscription gives the following genealogy of the Delhi rulers: Sāhavadina (Sihābbuddin), Ṣuduvadīna (Quṭbu'ddin Aibak), Samusadīna (Shamsuddin Iltutmish), Pherūjasāhi (Ruknuddin Firūz), Jalāladīna (Jalāluddin Razia), Maujadīna (Muizuddin Bahram), Alāvadīna (Alauddin Masud), Nasaradīna (Nasiruddin Mahmud), Śrī Hammīra Gayāsadīna (Ghiyasuddin Balban).

Similar genealogy is present in the Sarban stone inscription of AD 1378, found in the Raisina area of Delhi.[57] The object of this Sanskrit inscription too is to record the construction of a well in the vicinity of the village Saravala (Sarban) in the *pratigaṇa* of Indraprastha in the country of Hariyānā, for attainment of heaven by deceased ancestors, by two merchant brothers. The record contains a short genealogy of this merchant family from Agrataka (*Vaṇijam-Agrotaka-nivāsināṃ*). The second genealogy, of succession of rule, also relates to the country (*deśa*) of Hariyānā which is comparable to heaven on earth. The city of Ḍhillī in that country, says the record, was built by the Tomaras: the Tomaras were succeeded by the Cāhamānas who were conscientious in looking after their subjects; 'then, Mleccha Sāhavadina, whose scorching might burnt the garden which was the family of his enemy, took the city by force. Since then the city has been enjoyed by the Turuṣkas, the current lord of the land being Śrī Mahaṃmadaśāhi.'[58] The city was taken by force which the Naraina stone inscription mentioned, written a year earlier (1327); but also falling in the reign of Muhammad bin Tughlaq,[59] describes as *nijabāhuvīrya*, i.e. 'might of his own arms'. The purpose of this epigraph too is to record the construction of a well, for the satisfaction of the ancestors, by a merchant of—as the *vaṃśavarṇanam* (genealogical) part of the record describes it—*Rohītaka-vaṃśa*,[60] at the village of Nāḍāyaṇa, located in the western direction of Indraprastha. This is in the great and virtuous province of Hariyānaka where Kṛṣṇa along with Pārtha wandered for the suppression of sin; in its city of Ḍhillī, sin is expelled through the chanting of the Vedas. And in this country, 'there is the famous king Mahamudasāhi, the crest jewel of all the rulers of the earth, who by the strength of his own arms, has crushed [his] enemies, and is the powerful Śaka Lord'.[61]

[57] P. Prasad, *Sanskrit Inscriptions*, pp. 27–31; J. Eggeling, 'Sarban Inscription in the Delhi Museum', *EI*, vol. I, 1892; repr., Delhi, 1983, pp. 93–5.

[58] This is a rough translation of the following part of the text:

Atha pratāpadahanadagdhāri-kula-kānanaḥ
Mlecchaḥ Sāhavadina-stāṃ Balena Jagṛhe purīm
Tataḥ prabhṛti bhuktā sā Turuṣkair-yāvad-adya puḥ
Śrī Mahammadaśāhis-tāṃ pāti saṃprati bhūpatiḥ.

P. Prasad's translation of this is somewhat unsatisfactory.

[59] P. Prasad, *Sanskrit Inscriptions*, pp. 22–7.

[60] *Rohītaka-vaṃśa,* obviously locating its origin in Rohitaka or Rohtak in Haryana, can possibly be identified with the merchant subcaste of the Rohatgis; P. Prasad, *Sanskrit Inscriptions*, p. 16.

[61] *Tatr-āsīn Mahamudasāhir-akhila-kṣoṇīśa-cūḍāmanir vikhyāto nija-bāhu-vīrya-dalit-ārātiḥ Śakendro Balī.*

The representation of the succession of rule,[62] in the country of Hariyānā and in the city of Indraprastha or Ḍhillīka[63] uses symbols, similes and motifs which are common in other Sanskrit inscriptions, including *praśastis,* of earlier and of the same period; the ruler of the Śaka, Turuṣka or Mleccha descent may be seen to fit into the same convention, and if there is a new element or trail associated with his rule, it has to be so modified as to conform to this convention. One evidence of this is seen in the way the royalty of the Śaka/Turuṣka/Mleccha ruler is expressed: as *nṛpa, nṛpati, nṛpati-vara, nāyaka, samrāṭ, pṛthvīndra,*[64] *bhūmipati, bhūpati,*[65] *mahārājadhirāja*[66] and *paramabhaṭṭāraka,*[67] ruling over his *vijaya-rājya.*[68] Second, the ruler's

[62] The succession of rule from Tomara, through Cāhamāna, to Śakendra or the ruler of the Śakas figures also in another stone inscription, possibly from Sonepat; P. Prasad. *Sanskrit Inscriptions*, pp. 15–18.

[63] Compare the evidence of Palam Baoli and other inscriptions from Delhi with that of *Vividha-tīrtha-kalpa* of Jinaprabhasūri, a Jaina text of the first half of the fourteenth century: 'Pattana was established by Vanarāja, the pearl of the Caukkada [Cāpotkaḍā, Cāvaḍā] dynasty in Vikarama 802 in Lākṣārāma in the region under the rule of king Aṇahilla. Seven kings of the Cāvaḍā dynasty reigned: Vanarāja, Yogarāja, Kṣemarāja, Bhuyagaḍa, Vajrasiṃha, Ratnāditya, and Sāmantasiṃha. Then eleven kings of the Chalukya dynasty reigned in that town: Mularāja, Cāmuṇḍarāja, Vallabharāja. Durlabharāja, Bhīmadeva, Karṇa, Jayasiṃhadeva, Kumārapāladeva, Ajayadeva, the younger Mūlarāja, and Bhīmadeva. Then reigned the kings in the Vāghelā years: Lavaṇaprasāda, Vīradhavala, Vīsaladeva, Arjuna. Sāraṅgadeva, and Karṇadeva. Then in Gujarat came the rule of the Sultans: 'Ala-ud-dina, etc. But Ariṣṭanemi Svāmī is worshipped in the same way today.' John E. Cort, tr., 'Twelve Chapters from the Guidebook to various Pilgrimage Places, the *Vividhafirthakalpa* of Jinaprabhasūri', in *The Clever Adulteress and Other Stories: A Treasury of Jain Literature*, ed. Phyllis Granoff, Oakville, New York and London, 1990, p. 246.

[64] These titles all appear in the Palam Baoli inscription.

[65] The title *Mahārājādhirāja* given to Sultan Mahmud Khalji figures in two inscriptions, dated 1437 and 1446, in Deogarh fort in UP: P. Prasad, *Sanskrit Inscriptions*, pp. 201–2.

[66] Palam Baoli and Sarban Inscriptions.

[67] *Parambhaṭṭāraka,* an epithet of the sovereign ruler, is used for Shamsuddin Iltutmish (1210–36) in Mahoba fort copperplate inscriptions from Uttar Pradesh; the dates on the inscriptions are AD 1227 on one side and 1234–50 on the other. P. Prasad, *Sanskrit Inscriptions*, p. 80.

[68] Note, in this context, the interesting passage in a fifteenth-century saledeed of a girl and her son from Tirhut in north Bihar: 'in Tirabhukti, which is protected by *Mahārājādhirāja,* the prosperous Bhairavasiṃhadeva a Nārāyaṇa against enemy kings like Nārāyaṇa against Kaṃsa, who is engaged in devotion to Śiva and is shining with all the insignia received through the favour and boon of the Sultan, the prosperous Alāvadina Śāha, the *Paramabhaṭṭāraka, Parameśvara:* supreme lord, *aśvapati:* the lord of horses, *Gajapati,* the lord of elephants, *narapati:* the lord of men and *rājatrayādhipati:* supreme lord of a triad of kings and the guardian of the east. . .'. Mahes Raj Pant, 'Six 15th- and 16th-century Deeds from Tirhut Recording the Purchase of Slaves', in *Recht, Staat*

sovereignty extends over the earth having the ocean as its girdle, and his conquests extend to all directions. Note, for example, how the kingdom of Śrī Hammīra Gayāsaṃdīna is described in Palam Baoli inscription of 1276.[69]

In his kingdom, abounding in benign rule, extending from Gauḍa to Gajjana, from the Dravida region and from the Setubandha (to the north) where the entire region was filled with inner content, the earth bore vernal floral charms produced by the rays of the innumerable precious stones and corals which dropped on it from the crowns of the bent heads of the rulers who came from every direction for his service.

He, whose legions daily traversed for a bath the earth both eastward to the confluence of the Ganges with the (Gaṅgāsāgara) and westward to the confluence of the Indus with the sea. . . .

When he went forth on a military expedition, the Gauḍas abdicated their glory; the Andhras through fear sought the shelter of holes; the Keralas forsook their pleasures; the Karṇāṭas hid themselves in caves; the Mahārāṣṭras gave up their places, the Gurjjaras resigned their vigour and the Lāṭas turned into Kirātas.

The earth being now supported by this sovereign, Śeṣa, altogether forsaking his duty of supporting the weight of the globe, has betaken himself to the great bed of Viṣṇu; and Viṣṇu himself, for the sake of protection, taking Lakshmī on his breast, and relinquishing all worries, sleeps in peace on the ocean of milk.

Established metaphors are invoked to represent military exploits as well as the stability of the kingdom of the Śaka/Turuṣka ruler, much in the same way as they would be described in the records of the other ruling dynasties of the period. The point about this is that the inscriptions were not necessarily representing only empirical reality or concrete events; what is to be noted is the selection of terms for representation of what the rulers were seen as upholding. Thus, the wealth which was acquired, was seen, in an inscription of the time of Sikandar Shah Lodi, as having been acquired by adhering to the correct principle (*nyāyenopārjita*); the ruler was thus one 'who was beloved of his subjects (*prajā*) and giver of joy to them'.[70] The representation of Turuṣka/Śaka/Yavana rulers as adhering to norms which had been in

---

und Verwaltung im Klassischen Indien (The State, the Law and Administration in Classical India), ed. Bernhard Kölver, München, 1997, pp. 164–5.

[69] Palam Baoli inscription, verses 6–11.

[70] These terms occur in a stone inscription dated 1491 in the collection of the Lucknow Museum. The inscription belongs to the time of Sikander Shah Lodi, the expressions relate to a minor family of rulers, which is called in the inscription as *Bhalīma-vaṃśa*. P. Prasad, *Sanskrit Inscriptions*, pp. 210–11.

The choice of particular expressions was designed to project the ruler as upholder of royal norms. The king was expected to keep his subjects happy, his wealth, lawfully acquired, was only the share he was entitled to as the protector of his subjects. See R.S. Sharma, *Aspects of Political Ideas and Institutions in Ancient India*, Delhi, 3rd revd. edn., 1991, Chap. 5.

existence earlier included other traits which they came to be endowed with. There was, apart from the usual Sanskritization of individual names and names of lineages,[71] the modification of the title Sultān to *Suratrāṇa* which gave it the literal meaning 'Saviour of Gods'.[72] This pattern of representation also makes intelligible the search for a lunar, Pāṇḍava lineage for a medieval Muslim ruler of Kashmir, or the projection of Śāhi Śrīmad-Akabbara (Akbar), in the sixteenth-century text *Bhānucandra-carita,* as Rāma.[73]

If these representations are seen as relevant for understanding one dimension of the culture and politics of the early medieval / medieval period, then reference may be made to some additional material, bearing on the process of internalization. The Sultan of Delhi, as we have seen, could be a *maharājadhirāja* and *parama-bhaṭṭāraka;* the Candella rulers Paramārdideva, Trailokyavarmadeva and Vīravarmmadeva were called *paramabhaṭṭāraka, mahārājadhirāja, parameśvara, paramamaheśvara śāhi-maharāja* in the Charkhari (Charkhari tahsil, Hamirpur district, Uttar Pradesh) copperplate inscription of 1289.[74] The Arabic term *āmir,* modified to Hammīra or Hamvīra, could both denote the 'alien' who was an adversary, as also a local ruler, who could subdue the alien Hammīra.[75] Sultān, transformed into *Suratrāṇa* could thus be appropriated by rulers claiming to be sovereign among Hindu kings (*Hindurāya-suratrāṇa*); the term deriving its connotation not from its literal meaning, but from what its original (*Sultān*) signified. The term *Hindurāya-suratrāṇa* is of Vijayanagara origin used along with numerous other titles, it was intended to project the Vijayanagar rulers as chiefs among Hindu *rāyas* or kings;[76] the selection of the particular suffix *'suratrāṇa'* to *Hindurāya*

[71] For example, the transformation, in Lalitpur stone inscription of 1424, discovered in Deogarh fort, of the term Ghori into *Gaurī-kula*, to which *Śrīmān-Mālava-Pālaka, Śaka-nṛpa, Sāhi* Ālaṃbhaka (Hoshang Shah Ghori of Malwa) belonged; P. Prasad, *Sanskrit Inscriptions*, pp. 183–99.

[72] Several short inscriptions at Qutb Minar in Delhi have the form *Śrī Sulatrāṇa* (P. Prasad, *Sanskrit Inscriptions*, pp. 18–21), but this may not be taken to suggest that the form *Suratrāṇa* was arrived at through some intermediary stages. From the very widespread occurrence of the term *Suratrāṇa,* in different parts of India, it would appear that it gained ready currency as the Sanskritic equivalent of Sultan.

[73] The text (l. 39) has the following:

Tathā tat pālayāmāsa śāhiḥ Śrīmad Akabbaraḥ
Nityā yath-aiva nāsmārsit Kauśaleyaṃ jano-khilaḥ.

M.R. Pant suggests that the form *Kauśaleya* (son of Kauśalyā) may have been used for reasons of metre.

[74] P. Prasad, *Sanskrit Inscriptions*, pp. 144–8.

[75] *Hammīramahākāvya* in Prabha, *Historical Mahākāvyas*, Chap. 9.

[76] E. Hultzsch, 'Hampe Inscription of Krishnaraya, Dated Śaka 1430', *EI*, vol. I, pp. 361–71. Chandra Prabha cites (*Historical Mahākāvyas*, p. 330 and fn.3) the evidence of

makes it represent exactly what it is intended to oppose: the political might of the *sultan*. The title, like some other titles denoting political power such as *Śāha*,[77] was thus not essentialized but could remain open for use among royalty in general.

VI

Turuṣkas / Śakas / Mlecchas, depicted as shouldering the great burden of the earth (*mahābhāra*),[78] to the extent of relieving Viṣṇu of his worries,[79] is one kind of representation. In another kind, they themselves become the great burden of the earth, and the ruler who subdues them becomes comparable to Viṣṇu: this is a complete reversal of the former representation. Note, for example, the following reference to Candella Trailokyavarmadeva, father of Vīravarman, in Ajaigarh Fort Rock inscription of 1261 of the time of Vīravarman: 'Then Trailokyavarman, protector of the earth, who knew well how to provide for forts, ruled; like Viṣṇu he was, in lifting up the earth, immerged in the ocean formed by the streams of Turuṣkas.'[80]

The earth submerged by the Turuṣkas / Mlecchas is a regular motif, which is used to underline the significance of its rescue. The motif related to the perception of a changed order, of departure from what is familiar and held valuable, and, at times, of surrender to current reality, and, at other times, of positive action. The attitude of surrender to what is perceived as a changed order is expressed, with great pathos and faith in miracle, in an inscription written towards the close of the twelfth century and found at Etawah fort in

---

an inscription from Kolar district in Karnataka to show that the title *Hindurāya-suratrāṇa* dates to the time of Bukka I. Evidence of the use of the term *Hiṃdu-suratrāṇa* by a ruler of north India is provided by the Sadadi (west Rajasthan) inscription of 1439 of Guhila Rāṇā Kumbhakarṇa; he is mentioned as having received the title after defeating the Sultans of Ḍhillī and Gūrjaratrā. The title *Suratrāṇa* in this record is used with reference to Allāvadīna who was a contemporary and defeated adversary of Kumbhakarṇa's predecessor Bhuvanasiṃha; D.R. Bhandarkar, 'A List of Inscriptions of Northern India in Brahmi and its Derivative Scripts, from about 200 AC', *Appendix to Epigraphia Indica and Record of the Archaeological Survey of India*, vols. 19–23, Delhi, repr., 1983, pp. 109–10, no. 784. Sec. in this connection, the interesting discussion in Phillip B. Wagoner, '"Sultan among Hindu Kings": Dress, Titles, and the Islamicization of Hindu Culture at Vijayanagara', *Journal of Asian Studies*, vol. 55, pt. 4, 1996, pp. 851–80.

[77] See *Rastrauḍhavaṃśa-mahākāvyam*.

[78] Lucknow Museum Stone inscription, see n. 70.

[79] Palam Baoli inscription.

[80] The translation is slightly modified from what is available in F. Kielhorn, 'Two Chandella Inscriptions from Ajaygadh', *EI*, vol. I, p. 329.

Uttar Pradesh.[81] The inscription is of *mahārāja* Ajayasiṃha who, the record claims, was a nephew of the Gāhaḍavāla ruler Jayaccandra. The inscription states that *mahārāja* Ajayasiṃha and his *ācārya* and priest performed a *mahāyoga* of Caṇḍikā. It also refers to the installation, made earlier, of an image of Durgā, but 'now, with great sorrow, touching her with my head, I place this Durgā, the dweller of the fort and destroyer of bad luck into this pit, till the God Skanda turns their (of the Mlecchas) glory (sun) to dust. When ill fate meets Yavanas, she might reappear, or manifest herself again amidst uproar.'[82]

It has been mentioned before that the perception of the violation of an existing order, by 'violent and vile' Yavanas who harassed Gods and Brāhmaṇas, the important symbols of that order, is present in the Kharepatan plate of 1095 of the Śilāhāras of Konkan. The perception, more vividly expressed, and sometimes using the motif of the submergence of the earth, because of Mleccha domination, is present in records from thirteenth to fourteenth centuries. I cite excerpts from literary and epigraphic records of the period, both to illustrate how several images were made to converge in the literary idiom, and to make the point about counter-representation clearer.

The first reference I make is to *Madhurā-vijaya*, which, as mentioned earlier, was a *Mahākāvya* written by Gaṅgādevī, in the second half of the fourteenth century, in celebration of the victory of her husband Kampana over the Turuṣkas of Madurai. The narration,[83] providing an elaborate commentary on the nature of Turuṣka rule in Madurai, is done by a mysterious lady, the gift of a sword by whom enables Kampana in the end to kill the Turuṣka ruler:

> Vyāghrapurī had truly become the inhabitance of tigers where men lived formerly; the dome of the central shrine had become so dilapidated that it was only the hood of Ādiśeṣa that protected the image of Raṅganātha from falling. The Lord of Gajāraṇya, who is said to have killed an elephant to obtain its skin for a garment, was reduced lo a similar condition because of its being deprived of clothes.[84]

[81] P. Prasad, *Sanskrit Inscriptions*, pp. 92–3.

[82] Ibid. Inscriptions also refer to installation of new images to replace broken images. One can cite in this context the evidence of a Kiradu (west Rajasthan) inscription of 1178–9 which records the installation of an image by the wife of a subordinate official Tejapāla working under Mahārājaputra Madanabrahma, ruler of Kirāṭa-kūpa (Kiradu), during the time of Caulukya Bhīmadeva, to replace an image broken by the Turuṣkas. D.R. Bhandarkar, 'A List of Inscriptions', p. 56, no. 381.

[83] The citations made here are not extracts from the translation of the text; they are paraphrases, taken from publications cited further.

[84] Prabha, *Historical Mahākāvyas*, p. 339.

The continuation of the narrative is in a similar vein:

The temples in the land have fallen into neglect as worship in them has been stopped. Within their walls the frightful howls of jackals have taken the place of the sweet reverberations of the *mridanga*. Like the Turushkas who know no limits, the Kaveri has forgotten her ancient boundaries and brings frequent destruction with her floods. The sweet odour of the sacrificial smoke and the chant of the Vedas have deserted the villages (*agraharas*) which are now filled with the foul smell of roasted flesh and the fierce noises of the ruffianly Turushkas. The suburban gardens of Madura present a most painful sight; many of their beautiful coconut palms have been cut down; and on every side are seen rows of stakes from which swing strings of human skulls strung together. The Tamraparni is flowing red with the blood of the slaughtered cows. The Veda is forgotten and justice has gone into hiding; there is not left any trace of virtue or nobility in the land and despair is writ large on the faces of the unfortunate Draviḍas.[85]

The calamity, of which man and nature are both perceived to be agents, is made to be of cosmic proportions, and this is what links it up with the image of the recovery of the earth which became submerged in the ocean as a result of Mleccha rule, entitling its rescuer identity with the Primeval Boar (*Mahā-Varāha*). The Annavarappadu plates of 1385 and 1401, from the West Godavari district of Andhra Pradesh, refer to king Vema of the Reḍḍi family as having been 'praised as the Primeval Boar [*Mahā-Varāha*] by all the learned for his act of lifting up the country that was submerged under the *Mleccha* . . . ocean; the land of the Andhra shone brilliantly, and while this king was lawfully ruling [the earth], there flourished all the *śāstras* and Vedas and hundreds of sacrifices were performed'.[86]

'Blinding blackness, to which the earth passed' afflicted by the Turuṣkas, is another metaphor to underscore the calamity of Mleccha rule. It is used in another inscription from Andhra, the Vilasa grant of Prolaya Nāyaka, discovered near Pithapuram in East Godavari district and dated to about AD 1330.[87] The record is a detailed representation of a calamity, with its locus in a region, but with the region perceived as an integral component of a cosmological whole. The grant begins with invocations to Viṣṇu and his Varāha incarnation. This is followed by an account of the story of creation, going on to the description of Jambudvipa, comprising nine *Khaṇḍas*. Of these, the *Khaṇḍa* lying between the Himalaya and the southern ocean was Bhāratavarṣa—a country characterized by different languages and customs

[85] K.A. Nilakanta Sastri, *The Pandyan Kingdom: From the Earliest Times to the Sixteenth Century*, Madras; repr. 1972, p. 213.

[86] K.H.V. Sarma and T. Krishnamurty, 'Annavarappadu Plates of Kataya Vema Reddi', *EI*, vol. 36, pp. 167–90.

[87] N. Venkataramanayya and Somasekhara Sharma, 'Vilasa Grant'.

and in which 'deeds done produce fruits'; and, further, the country is divided into many countries (*phalaṃti karmāṇi kṛtāni yatra/Bhāṣā-samācāra-bhida-vibhinnair-deśair-anekair-bahudhā-vibhakte*). Tiliṅga, or Andhra—a land of many sacred rivers, rich towns and cities, beautiful mountains and other similar features—was ruled by kings of Solar and Lunar dynasties. In the Kali age, the Kākatis ruled the country from their capital Ekaśila, like the Ikṣvākus from Ayodhyā, and when Pratāparudra of the Kākati family ruled, even such celebrated rulers of the past as Yayāti, Nābhāga and Bhagīratha were completely forgotten:

While king Pratāparudra was ruling the kingdom in this manner, bitter hostility arose between him and Ahammada *suratrāṇa,* the lord of the Turushkas. The *suratrāṇa,* who was the Yama (Death) to the kings, stamped out the remnants of the royal families left undestroyed by Jāmadagnya (Paraśurāma). Although Pratāparudra vanquished that *suratrāṇa* who had an army of 9,000 horses seven times, he had to submit to the Turuṣka at last . . . owing to the decrease of the good fortunes of the people of the earth . . . when the Sun, viz., Pratāparudra set, the world was enveloped in the Turuṣka darkness. The evil (*adharma*), which he had up to that time kept under check, flourished under them, as the conditions were very favourable for its growth. The cruel wretches subjected the rich to torture for the sake of their wealth. Many of their victims died of terror at the very sight of their vicious countenances; the Brāhmaṇas were compelled to abandon their religious practices; the images of the Gods were overturned and broken; the *agrahāras* to the learned confiscated; the cultivators were despoiled of the fruits of their labour, and their families were impoverished and ruined. None dared to lay claim to anything, whether it was a piece of property or one's own life. To those despicable wretches wine was the ordinary drink, beef the staple food and the slaying of the Brāhmaṇas the favourite pastime. The land of Tiliṅga, left without a protector, suffered destruction from the Yavanas, like a forest subjected to devastating wild fire.

King Prola of the Musunūri family of the fourth or the Śudra varṇa, the grant goes on to state, destroyed the power of these Yavanas and re-established order in society:

The very people who suffered at the hands of the Yavanas sought protection under him, and turned against them and put them to death. Having overcome the Yavanas in this fashion, he restored to Brāhmaṇas their ancient *agrahāras* confiscated by them, and revived the performance of the sacrifices, the smoke issuing from the firepits of which spreading over the countryside cleared it of the pollution caused by the movements of those evil-doers. The agriculturists surrendered willingly a sixth of the produce of the soil to the king; and he set his hand to the task of repairing the damages caused by the Pārasīkas.

The *Madhurā-vijaya* and the epigraphic records from Andhra that I have cited all talk about calamity; in addition to other traits of disorder, the calamity takes the form of an end to the recitation of the Vedas, destruction and neglect of temples, decline of the settlements of the Brāhmaṇas and so on. The Vilasa grant describes the collapse of an ideal social order in comprehensive terms, and the above traits arc the chief traits of the order which is restored: this is a feat comparable to the lifting of the earth submerged in the ocean. It is a feat highlighted by portraying the magnitude of the calamity, of the total destruction of what is perceived as valuable in society, brought about by the rule of the Yavanas.

The description of the devastation, whether portrayed in the *Madhurā-vijaya* or the Vilasa grant will be, and has been, commonly taken to represent the one and exclusive reality of Yavana rule; the return to the old order, similarly, is taken to represent the reality of a liberation. It needs to be seen, however, that the image of the Turuṣka/Yavana *suratrāṇa* and of his community as the destroyer of the existing social order is what may be called counter-representation of the *suratrāṇa* as the perpetuator of that social order, or vice versa. The event of Yavana victory and rule is a reality, but the reality, as the Palam Baoli inscription and the Vilasa grant show, could be represented in two ways. In one representation, the destroyer of the Yavana who is a destroyer of social order is comparable to Viṣṇu; in another, Yavana, as a benign ruler, gives succour to Viṣṇu who, leaving the burden of preservation to the ruler, retires to peaceful sleep in the ocean of milk. It cannot be argued that chronologically one representation replaces the other. The Yavanas of Kharepatan plate (AD 1095) were 'violent and vile', so were the Yavanas of *Madhurā-vijaya* and the Vilasa grant. But, if the Rāṣṭrakūṭa plates of early tenth century from Chinchani wished that the rule of the Yavana ruler Śrī Sugatipa, of the prowess of the Sun (*Sūryatejāḥ*) continued (*praśastu*),[88] the Kangra Jwalamukhi *praśasti* from north India, written between 1433 and 1446, also wished the fame (*kīrtti*) of Śrīmad Śāhi-Mahammada, the ruler of Delhi, to be victorious.[89] The Lord of Delhi (*Dillīśvara*) in the period of the Mughals could be seen as performing different roles: he could both be a support to what is described as *a Rāmarājya* (*varṇyate tasya rājyam hi Rāmarājyopamam śubham*);[90] as one comparable to Rāma, the lord of Delhi could himself be

[88] Sircar, 'Rashtrakuta Charters from Chinchani'.

[89] G. Bühler, 'The Kangra Jwalamukhi Prasasti', *EI*, vol. I, pp. 190–5.

[90] This is how the kingdom of Durgabhānu, a local Chandrawat ruler of Mandasor, has been described in an inscription of the early seventeenth century. The Candrawat rulers claimed to have obtained many countries from the *Dillīśvara*, 'Lord of Delhi' (*Dillīśvarāt-prāpta . . . deśān-anekān*): Sadhu Ram, 'Two Inscriptions from Rampura, Samvat 1664', *EI*, vol. 36, pp. 121–30.

seen as a ruler of *Rāmarājya*.[91] The representations of Yavana rule can thus be seen to constitute a contradiction, the origin of which needs to be explained. This is a problem which will be taken up in the concluding chapter after I present material of another kind in the next.

[91] *Bhānucandra-carita*, 1.39.

CHAPTER 3

Meritorious Deeds, Sacred Sites and the Image of God as the Lord of the Universe

I begin this chapter with a reference to the *Carita* of Jagaḍū, the famed merchant of Sola *Kula,* also called *Śrīmalavaṃśa,* who, according to Jaina texts, was a contemporary of Lavaṇaprasāda and Vīsaladeva, Caulukya-Vāghela rulers of Gujarat in the thirteenth century.[1] Like Vastupāla and Tejaḥpāla,[2] ministers of the Vāghela rulers, Jagaḍū too is portrayed as a merchant who controlled an extensive commercial network. Jagaḍū got the boon from Ratnākara, the Ocean deity, that his ships would always arrive safely at port. His subordinate Jayantasiṃha of Upakeśa lineage sailed with ships laden with goods across to Ārdrapura or Hormuz and encountered a Turuṣka (also called Śaka) merchant of Stambhapurī or Cambay in Gujarat, at that port. Obviously, the gains of commerce made Jagaḍū fabulously wealthy. *Jagaḍū-carita,* like the *Caritas* of Vastupāla, is however, not concerned primarily with mundane details of Jagaḍū's commercial career or with his mode of commerce and commercial links. It is concerned with the munificence and benefactions of Jagaḍū as a pious follower of Jaina faith, although it does not, at the same time, fail to highlight the valour of Jagaḍū by stating: 'With

[1] G. Bühler, *The Jagaḍūcharita of Sarvāṇanda, A Historical Romance from Gujarat,* Indian Studies, no. 1, Wien, 1892. For historicity of Jagaḍū or Jagadeva see, M. Shokoohy, *Bhadreśvar: The Oldest Islamic Monuments in India,* Leiden, 1988, pp. 8–10.

[2] Bhogilal J. Sundesara. *Literary Circle of Mahāmātya Vastupāla and Its Contribution to Sanskrit Literature,* Bombay, 1953.

the army of the Caulukya King, he conquered the irresistible Mudgalas, and, making apparent his valour, gave peace to the world.'[3]

Jagaḍū-carita makes special mention of two benefactions of Jagaḍū. One was the massive relief provided by him when the whole country was afflicted by a terrible famine. From his reportedly seven hundred well-filled granaries, grain was distributed to different rulers, the recipients being (*Jagaḍū-carita,* vi.123–37):

Vīsaladeva	8,000 *mūṭakas* (measure)
Hammīra, ruler of Sind	12,000
Madanavarman, ruler of Avantī	18,000
Garjaneśa, Mojadina, ruler of Delhi	21,000
Pratāpasiṃha, ruler of Kāśī	32,000
Skandhila, famed as an Emperor (*Cakrīkhyāti-bhṛt*)	12,000

Jagaḍū's other acts of munificence were mostly in the form of patronage to Jaina religious shrines, but also included the construction of a *masīti* (masjid) called Shīmālī, i.e. 'probably Ism'ali (the most high name)'.[4] When Jagaḍū's pious life came to an end, the news caused intense sadness in all quarters: 'When the neighbouring princes heard of his death, they all mourned for him. The king of Delhi (Garjanesa) took off his turban from his head, Arjuna wept loudly and the king of Sindh did not touch food during two days.'[5]

The 'facts' mentioned in the *Jagaḍū-carita* need not be taken at their face value; the *Carita,* like the 'literary circles' of Vastupāla, introduce to us the world of big merchants whose affluence could reach across to different political regimes and religious persuasions. *Jagaḍū-carita* is a text remarkably free from exclusivity; regimes and faiths are represented as many components of the same world in which Jagaḍū extended his munificence.

The deeds performed by other merchant families, or by individuals, of north India, also performed for the acquisition of merit, may not have been on the same scale, but they also tell us, as a significant complement to what other sources convey to us about this period, that these deeds are performed in a society which recognized and therefore recorded certain acts, irrespective of who performed them, as acts of merit. The Palam Baoli, Sarban, Naraina,

[3] Bühler, *Jaguḍūcharita,* pp. 18–19. The Mudgalas have been identified with Mongols who were undertaking regular raids into India in this period, see M. Habib and K.A. Nizami, eds., *A Comprehensive History of India,* vol. 5, *The Delhi Sultānat, AD 1206-1526,* Delhi, 1982, Chap. I.

[4] Bühler, *Jagaḍūcharita,* p. 18.

[5] Ibid., p. 22.

Chirkhane Ka Mandir and Delhi Museum inscriptions, referring to acts such as constructions of *dharmaśālā*, *vāpī* and *kūpa*, and installation of *Tirthaṃkara* by the merchant families of the Delhi-Haryana region, were statements of meritorious deeds performed with reference to the *Vijaya-rājya* of the Turuṣka/Śaka *nṛpati*.[6] It is in the context of such deeds and the underlying aspirations of the society of the particular locality that one can situate an inscription of a later period: the Mubarakpur-Kotla Persian-Sanskrit bilingual inscription of 1517. The Sanskrit part of the inscription refers to the victorious kingdom (*Vijaya-rājya*) of Suratrāṇa Śrī Bahalola-tanaya-pātisāha-Śrī Sikandara and goes on to record:

There was a person named Sekha Sikandara who belonged to the *Serātī* family (*gotra*) and was the son of Bājīda, son of Sekha Ahiā. His wife was Murādi Khātū who was the daughter of Dilāvara Khāna of the Saravāṇī family. Lady Āsā, daughter of Pātisāha Bahlola, and sister of Sikandara, caused a well to be excavated for the merit of the said Murādi (Murāde) and of herself.[7]

The reference to the *kūpa* (well), which is the Sanskrit of *imārat-i-chāh* of the Persian part of the inscription,[8] is not the only element which makes the statement about the event similar to the recording of such acts performed by the merchant families of Delhi-Haryana; the inscription attributes, by using terms like *gotra, puṇyārtham, ācandrārkaṃ naṃdatu māṃgalyaṃ bhavatu*, the same traits to the event of the construction of a well by Lodi Bibi 'Ayisha' (Bibi Śrī Āsā of the Sanskrit record) as would be associated with the construction of a well by merchant families, as mentioned before. The invocation of what is in consonance with convention and considered appropriate for the occasion can be similarly seen in a Qutb Minar inscription of 1369.[9] When the *minār*, mentioned in the record as *munāro*, was renovated during the reign of the illustrious Suratrāṇa Pherojasāhi, the record used the term *jīrṇoddhāra* (literally, 'restoring what exists in a state of ruin'); the work was done by *sūtradhāri* (architect) Cāhaḍa and by craftsmen (*Śilpī Sūtra*) Nānā and Sālhā, and the carpentry work (*dārukarma*) was done by Dharamuvānani. The record stresses that the work was completed through the grace of Śrī Viśvakarmā, the deity of architects and craftsmen. One of

[6] P. Prasad, *Sanskrit Inscriptions of Delhi Sultanate 1911–1526*, Delhi, 1990, pp. 3–18, 22–31, 35–6.

[7] Y.K. Bukhari, 'Inscriptions from the Archaeological Museum, Red Fort. Delhi', *Epigraphia Indica: Arabic and Persian Supplement* (In continuation of *Epigraphia Indo-Moslemica*), 1959-61, Delhi, 1987, no. 6. pp. 8–10; see also P. Prasad, *Sanskrit Inscriptions*.

[8] Ibid.

[9] M.C. Joshi, 'Some Nagari Inscriptions on the Qutb Minar', *Medieval India—A Miscellany*, vol. 2, Aligarh, 1972, pp. 3–6; P. Prasad, *Sanskrit Inscriptions*, pp. 33–5.

the editors of the record has commented that 'the reference to a Hindu deity in what is technically part of a mosque has an irony of its own',[10] but if there was no irony in the use of such terms as *gotra, puṇyārtha* and *ācandrārka* with reference to a meritorious deed by members of the Lodi family, then there was no irony either in the invocation of Viśvakarmā in what was seen as the *jīrṇoddhāra* of a *minār* by craftsmen who were *sūtradhāras, śilpīs* and workers in *dārukarma*.

Another Sanskrit inscription of the period of the Delhi Sultanate, found at a considerable distance from Delhi at Batihagarh,[11] 21 miles north-west of Damoh in Madhya Pradesh, may also be studied in this context. The inscription is dated in AD 1328. After invoking 'the Creator of all the worlds', '. . . whose power is subservient to his wish, who is unlimited, who has no beginning and no end, and who is destitute of quality and colour', the inscription goes on to refer to King Mahamuda Suratrāṇa.[12] Mahamuda is described as Śakendra and Vasudhādhipa, and as one who, having established himself at Yoginīpura (Delhi) ruled the whole earth. The inscription records that Jallāla Khojā, son of Iśākārāja, a local representative of the governor of that region, caused a *Gomaṭha* as well as a garden (*udyāna*) and step well (*vāpī*), to be made at Baṭihāḍim-pura. Described as a shelter for all animals (*āśrayaḥ-sarva-jantunām*), the *Gomaṭha*[13] was like another Kailāsa; the garden was like Nandana, and the *vāpī* resembled 'the disc of the spotless moon' and showered 'nectar of virtue'. While Jallāla Khojā's servant Dhanau, described as *svāmī-bhakta* (devoted to his lord) was put in charge of the establishment (*karmasthāne niyojitaḥ*), the work of construction was executed by *sūtradhāras* of auspicious Śilāpaṭṭa family, and the composition and preparation of the record, describing the work, were carried out by members of Māthura Kāyastha families.

The Batihagarh stone inscription makes it clear that the constructions of a *Gomaṭha* and a *vāpī*, and the laying out of a garden, brought the local ruler, who through a hierarchical chain presented himself as a representative of the ruler of Delhi, in close contact with different local social groups; they

[10] P. Prasad, *Sanskrit Inscriptions*.

[11] Hira Lal, 'Batihagarh Stone Inscription, Samvat 1385', *EI*, vol. 12, 1913–14, Delhi, repr. 1982, pp. 44–7.

[12] This ruler is identified with Nasīr-ud-dīn Mahmud (1246–66). It is curious that the inscription, dated much later than his period, should refer to him.

[13] The editor of the inscription does not explain what a *Gomaṭha* could have been. Mahes Raj Pant has suggested to me that it could mean a *go-śālā*—'a cattle-shed'. Interestingly, Batihadim where, according to the record, the *Gomaṭha* was constructed, 'in the local dialect means heap of a collection of cow-dung cakes', ibid., p. 45. Further, the inscription itself refers to the *go-maṭha* as 'the shelter for all animals'.

participated in different capacities in the execution of this meritorious deed which obviously was initiated by the local ruler. The record does not tell us what Jallāla Khojā's motivation was except to state that he considered 'his stock of religious merit in his mind' (*dharmma-puñjaṃ hi vicārya*); it would seem that he perceived this act of patronage as an appropriate mode of interaction with the local community.

What one can argue, with reference to the situation that I have been outlining, is that like political space composed of many contestants, other spaces too—such as religious—had a variety of components, including, perhaps, disparate and significantly dissimilar components as well. But the variety, by its very presence, in a society in which they had tangible meanings, generated different compulsions and not a predetermined, unilinear response. It is this heterogeneity of traits of a given situation, which needs to be kept in mind while trying to understand cases which, outwardly, may appear unusual or as cases of total mismatch. To illustrate this point further, to an inscription of 1424, discovered in the ruins of the old fort at Deogarh, near Jhansi in south Uttar Pradesh can be referred to.[14] Like several other inscriptions of this period from Deogarh, this inscription too is of Jaina affiliation and opens with an eulogy of Tirthaṃkara Vṛṣabha, also curiously mentioned as Sugata and Sadāśiva. It goes on to refer to a number of Jaina potentates and to the consecration of images of two of them, Padmanandi and Damavasanta, by one Holi.

The statements about Holi and his father, in combination with some elements in the language of the record, call for attention. Holi was the son of Sāhi Ālaṃbhaka by his wife Ambikā. Ālaṃbhaka, a name Sanskritized from Alp Khān, more commonly known as Sultan Hoshang Shāh Ghori, is said to have made the *Gaurīkula* (Ghori lineage) prosperous, was *Śrīmān-Mālava-pālaka* and *Śaka-nṛpa,* and when setting out on his victory campaign, he started from Maṇḍapapura (Mandu). Holi dedicated the images with the assistance of Guṇakīrtti, Harapati, Varddhamāna, Nandana, Sunandana and others; he was a *sādhu,* he was also *saṃgheśvara* or *saṃghādhipa* (Lord of the Jaina congregation). The linguistic element in the record, which has been especially commented upon by one of its editors, is the use of words in double meanings, in addition to the extended use of Sugata and Sadāśiva, non-Jaina epithets, for Jaina Tirthaṃkara Vṛṣabha. The use of words in a double sense is seen to be a practice of the epics and of Hindu mythology;

thus well known proper names such as Rāma (God) also means delight and rejoicing in beauty, and Arjuna has the alternative meaning of white. Varddhamāna has used Bhīma, Sahadeva, Balrāma [*sic*] and Yudhiṣṭra [*sic*] in similar ways to denote double

[14] Prasad, *Sanskrit Inscriptions*, pp. 183–99.

meanings. The technique is very common in Sanskrit literature; but its frequent and correct use in this inscription, which was written under a Muslim ruler, is a fact of extreme interest.

From the point of view of the composition of the text, what is really of interest is that it represents a conjunction of diverse elements: Jaina, Brahmanical and Sanskritized Islamic. The conjunction is illustrative of one pattern, out of a possible range of patterns, and of linkage and interaction between cultural elements, the diversity of which constituted the social and ideological situation of this period.

II

The *Jagaḍū-carita* and other evidence cited earlier point not to sharp polarity as the only and inevitable pattern of religiosity, but also to other possible ways in which social and ideological elements could combine in different local contexts and in different historical situations. Meritorious deeds, socially defined, and not simply in terms of normatively defined urge for the transcendental alone, can be seen to have brought together apparently irreconciliable elements as sponsors of an act of patronage. Further, the different elements of a historical situation, and not a single element alone, need to be studied in relation to that situation. The trend of convergence, when one looks at possible patterns of interaction between different elements, may be seen to manifest itself more clearly when a religious centre, with a local/regional base, emerges as a centre of common focus. Going backward chronologically from the period of the sources I have been discussing, the set of Chinchani plates, from the Dahanu taluk in Thane, Mumbai, dating to the ninth–early tenth centuries,[15] constitute the kind of evidence which can provide some insight into this process. It has already been mentioned that the Chinchani plates of the Rāṣṭrakūṭa period refer to the Tājika ruler (*nṛpati*) Madhumati Sugatipa of *Saṃyāna maṇḍala* which Sugatipa received through the grace of Rāṣṭrakūṭa rular Kṛṣṇarāja (*Kṛṣṇarāja-dayāvāpta-kṛtsna-Saṃyāna maṇḍala*). The plates which are records of religious benefaction in the locality of Saṃyāna in this period, record several provisions made by Madhumati Sugatipa. One, he established 'free ferry on two streams (near Saṃyāna, apparently on the Samyan river) and also a feeding house (at Saṃyāna) where Śāli rice, curries and ghee were catered free of cost'.[16] The second provision was of the form of a grant of land to a newly established *maṭhikā*, i.e. a monastic establishment of modest proportions.

[15] D.C. Sircar, 'Rashtrakuta Charters from Chinchani', *EI*, vol. 32, Delhi, repr. 1987.

[16] Ibid., p. 47.

The *maṭhikā* was constructed by one Annaiya, a brāhmaṇa of Bhāradvāja *gotra* and Maitrāyanī *śākhā*, and a friend of Puvvaiya, Sugatipa's minister. On request from Annaiya, Madhumati Sugatipa made a grant of the village of Kāṇāḍuka situated in Kolimahāra Viṣaya of Saṃyāna *maṇḍala,* together with another plot of land in the village of Devīhara; the endowments were made with the permission of the overlord Paramabhaṭṭāraka, Mahārājadhirāja, Parameśvara Indrarājadeva. The grant was to ensure repairs of the *maṭhikā;* for the offering of *naivedya* to the goddess Daśamī possibly enshrined in the *maṭhikā;* and for the feeding of nine persons belonging to the Pañca-Gauḍīya-Mahāparsad of Saṃyāna. The creation of a rent-free holding having been the prerogative of a ruler; this was done by Madhumati with the permission of his overlord and by making a declaration regarding the creation of the endowment at an assembly of the *Haṃyamana-pauras,*[17] Dhruvas and *Viṣayik-ādhikārikas*—representatives of communities and officials—of Saṃyāna. The grant, which the record describes as the *dharma-setu,* i.e. 'bridge of *dharma'*[18] was to last for ever, and its creator Śrī Sugatipa-*nṛpati,* whose *tejaḥ* equalled that of the Sun, was to continue to rule (*dattem yeneha so Śrī Sugatipa-nṛpati Sūryatejaḥ praśastu*).

The Tājikas, the community to which Sugatipa belonged, did not continue to rule for long in the Konkan region; it is known that Cāmuṇḍarāja, a feudatory of the Śilāhāra ruling family of the region, became the ruler of Saṃyāna *pattana* before 1034.[19] The *maṭhikā,* to which land was assigned by Sugatipa and which had come to be known as Kauṭuka *maṭhikā* after the name of the brother of its founder, continued to flourish, despite some nagging land dispute between the shrine of its goddess and an adjacent shrine of another deity, Madhusūdana.[20] It also continued to receive support of the local ruler and the local community. *Mahāmaṇḍaleśvara* Cāmuṇḍarāja,

[17] Opinions sharply differ on the meaning of the term *Haṃyamana,* which is sometimes taken to denote the community of Parsees of western India. See Sircar, 'Rashtrakuta Charters from Chinchani', p. 48. However, V.V. Mirashi is of the opinion that *Haṃyamana* corresponds to Kannada *haṃyamāna,* meaning artisans; V.V. Mirashi, *Inscriptions of the Śilāhāras, Corpus Inscriptions Indicarent,* vol. 6, Delhi, 1997, p. 58, n. 8. Parsee association with Konkan area in early eleventh century is suggested by a few Pahlavi inscriptions at the cave site of Kunheri, in Mumbai: Shobhana Gokhale, *Kanheri Inscriptions,* Pune, 1991, pp. 142–6.

[18] It is interesting to recall that the cave-shelter for the Buddhist *saṅgha* built on a Nasik hill by Gautamīputra Śātakarṇi' smother was described by Gautamīputra's son Vāsiṣṭhiputra Puḷumāvi when he made some endowment to the monks residing at the shelter, as *dharma-setu.* D.C. Sircar, *Select Inscriptions Bearing on Indian History and Civilization,* vol. I, 2nd edn., Calcutta, 1965, p. 205.

[19] D.C. Sircar, "Three Grants from Chinchani', *EI,* vol. 32, pp. 61–76.

[20] Ibid., pp. 64–5. See also Mirashi, *Inscriptions of the Śilāhāras,* pp. 71–5.

another Chinchani record of 1034 tells us, made a grant of a *ghāṇaka* or oil mill in favour of the Kauṭuka *maṭhikā*; this was to provide for the burning of a lamp for the goddess enshrined in the monastery and for 'besmearing oil on the feet of the *svādhyāyikas* or scholars apparently belonging to the *mahāparṣad* attached to the *maṭhikā* and of the brāhmaṇa visitors to the *maṭhikā*'.[21] The order of the grant was communicated to Cāmuṇḍarāja's subordinates and representatives of the local community: to the elders of the *Haṃyamana,* to courtiers and such officials as Alliya, Mahāra and Madhumata; to Śreṣṭhis Keśari, Suvarṇa, Kakkala who were *paura-mukhyas;* to merchants Uva, Suvarṇa and Somaiya; to Viṣayī Verthalaiya; to *śālā-sthāna-mukhya* Yājñikara; to Kṣita, Limbaiya, Velaiya, etc., who were also Viṣayīs; and to Agasti, Sīluva, Gavī, Bhāskara, Arjuna, etc., who were members of the *mahāparṣad* of the *maṭhikā.* Alliya, Mahāra and Madhumata, *Mahāmaṇḍaleśvara* Cāmuṇḍarāja's *saṃvyavaharikas,* bore, it has been pointed out, Arabic names, as did Madhumati Sugatipa, the *nṛpati* of the area in the period of Rāṣṭrakūṭa Kṛṣṇa II and Indra III. To the composer of the record, it was in the order of things to refer to them only as several representatives of a heterogenously constituted local community which was associated with an act of religious benefaction. The history of the Kauṭuka *maṭhikā* is not available beyond this date, but the pattern of relationship between local rule, local community and a local religious centre, as suggested by its available history, may be looked for in other locations, at other times.

III

Meritorious deeds, whether performed by individuals or families, or performed in the context of a larger social base, are known to us since they were recorded; the purpose obviously was, as it earlier was, communication of the significance of the act being performed; the recorded deeds were in consonance with what could be practised, despite sharply articulated differences in a situation of antagonistic ideological strands. Relevant to the theme of the present chapter, perhaps the most elaborate record of a meritorious act available for analysis so far, is the Veraval (Gujarat) record of AD 1264,[22] of the time of the Caulukya-Vāghela ruler Arjunadeva who ruled between 1261 and 1274. I shall attempt a detailed reference in this section to this record, relating it to the theme of the present work. In some ways my understanding of this record differs from what has been suggested by others earlier; I shall point them out at appropriate places.

[21] Ibid.

[22] D.C. Sircar, 'Veraval Inscriptions of Chaulukya-Vaghela Arjuna, 1264 AD', *EI*, vol. 34, 1961–2, Delhi, 1963.

The Chinchani records from Saṃyāna *pattana* relate to a *maṭhikā* and the shrine of a goddess; the Veraval record, originally from Somanātha *pattana*, another port town but located further north, in Kathiawar peninsula, relates to the construction of a mosque. The record is in two languages, Sanskrit and Arabic. Although the Arabic text is taken to be the Arabic version of the Sanskrit record, there are some significant differences between the two texts; one can assume that the Arabic version was not really intended for communication within the entire local community of Somanātha *pattana*, but for the Arab community alone.[23] However, although the Arabic version was prepared two months later than the Sanskrit text, particulars about the construction of the mosque are similar in the two records.[24]

Briefly, the following is what the record tells us about the construction of the mosque (*mijigiti*). The *mijigiti*, which the record calls a *dharmasthāna*, i.e. 'a site for religion' was constructed by *Nākhudā* (Captain or Commander of a ship) Noradīna Pīroja (Nuruddin Firuz), son of Khojā Nākhudā Abu Ibrahim of Hurmuja *deśa* (Hormuz). Nuruddin Firuz had come to Somanāthadeva *pattana* when *āmir* Ruknuddin was governing the harbour of Hormuz. This was, in Gujarat, during the reign of *Parameśvara, Paramabhaṭṭāraka, mahārājadhirāja* Arjunadeva; *rāṇaka* Mahādeva was, during this time, *mahāmātya*, and the *pancakula* at Somanāthadeva *pattana* was headed by Para (*Purohita*) Vīrabhadra, an *ācārya* of Śaiva Pāśupata doctrine and Abhayasiṃha, an important member of the local mercantile community. Through the help of local residents, *Nākhu* Noradīna Pīroja acquired a piece of land on which he was entitled to undertake any work (*yatheṣṭa-karma-karaṇīyatvena*) and which was located at Mahājanapālī in Sikottarī, mentioned as lying outside Somanāthadeva *nagara*. Noradīna Pīroja, attached to his faith (*dharma-bāndhava*), used this plot of land to construct a *mijigiti* (mosque) which the inscription, as mentioned earlier, describes as a *dharmasthāna*.

I believe that there are two major points about the way the construction of the mosque, its highlighted significance for the local community within which the mosque was sited, and the provisions made for the mosque, have been represented in the text of the Veraval record. One bears upon its network. The plot of land on which the mosque was constructed was located outside Somnath, but its network linked it both to royal administration and to representatives of local society. The acquisition of the plot of land was governed by the principle of *nava-vidhāna* and *sparśana* which put it

[23] For an impression of significant presence of Arab and Persian communities in Gujarat in the Vāghela period see Z.A. Desai, 'Muslims in the 13th century Gujurat, as Known from Arabic Inscriptions', *Journal of Oriental Institute*, vol. 10, Baroda, 1960–1, pp. 353–64.

[24] Sircar, 'Veraval Inscription', p. 145.

in the category of gift lands for which taxes had to be paid. The land was secured from a person referred to in the record as Bṛha Rāja Chāḍā, son of Rāja Nānasiṃha, in the presence of all the *Jamāthas* (possibly, Muslim congregations) and prominent persons who were labelled *Bṛhatpuruṣa Rāja, Bṛhatpuruṣa ṭha(kkura), Bṛhatpuruṣa rāṇaka*—different appellations but obviously together constituting the elites of the society. When certain grants were made in favour of the mosque, for observance of religious rites and for its proper maintenance, they consisted of: (1) *pallaḍikā* belonging to God Vakuleśvaradeva, consisting of houses facing different directions; they were situated in Somanāthadeva *nagara* and secured from priests, respectively of the temples of Navaghaneśvara and Ratneśvara; (2) another *pallaḍikā* or property of a *maṭha*; (3) one oilmill; and (4) two *haṭṭas,* located in front of the mosque, and secured, again, from important persons of the locality in which the mosque was located. The management of the property and the *āyapada* (i.e. income) of the mosque, the record specifies, was to be the concern of the (1) the congregation of *nākhudā-nāvikas,* owners or commanders of ships and sailors; (2) congregation of the *ghāṃcikas* or the oilmen of the town, together with their *khatiba* or preacher; (3) congregation of *chūṇakaras* or whitewashes; and (4) congregation of *Musalamānas* among the *patrapatis,* probably referring to those who drove horse carts in the town. The use of the term *samasta-śahara* in the record, which is taken to mean the entire city of Somanāthadeva *nagara*, possibily signified the space from which members were intended to be drawn for the proper upkeep and functioning of the mosque. Though located outside the limits of the town, in terms of its spatial as well as human network, the mosque thus did expand into the town of Somanāthadeva *nagara* it was a part of the cultural-religious horizon of that locality.

Before I take up the second point in the record about the mosque, I would like to refer to another aspect of the network of the mosque. While dwelling on the *āyapada* of the mosque, the record stipulates that 'whatever surplus remains (in the hands) of those who make payments out of the said income (or its source) for the upkeep and maintenance of the place of worship (i.e. the mosque) and for the expense of particular festivals and that of holy occasions should have to be sent to the places of worship at Makhā (Mecca) and Madīnā (Medina)'. D.C. Sircar, who re-edited the inscription recently, offered the following comment on this provision: 'It is interesting that Nūruddīn Fīrūz did not think of spending the surplus amount in some good cause in the land where the mosque was built but arranged for its dispatch to distant Mecca and Medina.'[25] This comment, however, seems to completely

[25] Ibid.

miss out on the cultural-religious logic of this particular provision. To Fīrūz, the provision could not follow from concern about the welfare of the land in which the mosque was built. As *a paramadhārmika,* i.e. as a devoutly religious person who followed the meanings of the codes of his own *dharma* (*svadharmaśāstrābhiprāyeṇa*), the mosque that he constructed was simply a representative of the apex *dharmasthānas* at Makhā (Mecca) and Madīnā (Medina). The dispatch of what remained as surplus to Mecca and Medina (*Makhā-Madīnā-dharmasthāne*) was a way of ensuring greater sanctity and legitimacy for his mosque by linking it to the apex *dharmasthānas* of his faith.[26]

The second major point about the record relates to the meanings attributed to the act of the construction of the mosque and to the mosque itself by the composer of this Sanskrit record, who however remains unnamed. The mosque was a *dharmasthāna,* as were, as already mentioned, Makhā and Madīnā. The construction of the mosque was undertaken by Firuz for achieving fame and renown, to last as long as the sun and the moon, and for his own welfare (*ā-candrārka-sthāyinī-kīrti-prasiddhyārtham-ātmanaḥ śreyo 'rtham*). The mosque faced the east (*pūrvābhimukha*). The religious performances at the mosque consisted of daily worship and had provisions of light, oil and drinks (*pratidinaṃ pūjā-dīpa-taila-pānīyārtham*); readings and prayers by *mālima* (Arabic *muallim,* 'an instructor'), *modina* (Arabic *muazzin,* a public crier to prayers), and a monthly reader (of the holy Koran); and particular religious festivals (*pūjā-mahotsava*) like *Barātiśabi-khatamarātri* (*Shab-i-barāt*) 'in accordance with the custom (*samācara*) of the leaders or owners of ships (*nau-vittaka*)'.[27]

The juxtaposition of terms such as *pūjā, dīpa, taila, mahotsava* which are used in the context of temple rituals with Arabic terms for Islamic religious observances and rituals is in keeping with the way the mosque was being represented as a *dharmasthāna.* Since this was a *dharmasthāna,* the grants made to it by Firuz for the observance of religious rites and for its upkeep were done

[26] D.C. Sircar does not mention in the editorial introduction to the record that the surplus was not in the form of money; it was in the form of what is called *dravya* which remained in excess from special festivals; the record says: *Tathā viśeṣa mahotsava-parva-vyaye kurvatāṃ ca yat-kiñcit śeṣa-dravyam-udgīrati tat sarvaṃ dravyaṃ Makhā-Madīnā-dharma-sthāne prasthāpanīyam,* ibid., p. 149, lines 35–7. Macca and Madīnā were indeed reference points for the devout located in India. Baton refers to an inscription of 1567 on the congregational mosque in Old Malda, in Bengal, which compared 'it with the holy shrine in Mecca, referring to Malda's house of worship as the "second Ka'aba" (*thani Ka'aba*)'. Richard M. Eaton, *The Rise of Islam and the Bengal Frontier, 1204–1760,* Delhi, 1994, p. 100.

[27] Sircar, 'Veraval Inscription', p. 144.

with libations of water (*udakena pradattam*). Protecting the *dharmasthāna* and making and maintaining grants to it were acts of merit (*puṇya-karma*), entitling their performer passage to heaven (*svargga-gāminaḥ*). Those who did the reverse were of sinful soul (*pāpātmā*); their acts were identical to committing five great sins (*panca-mahāpātaka-doṣa*) and made them go to hell (*naraka-gāmī*).[28] The representation of the mosque in the image of the sacred centres of the contemporary period[29] is a reflection of the manner in which Divinity too is conceived in the record. The record which begins with an auspicious *siddham* symbol has next an invocation, by the author of Viśvanātha (*Oṃ namaḥ Śrī Viśvanāthāya*). Śrī Viśvanātha (literally, 'Lord of the Universe') is Śiva, who as Somanātha, is the presiding deity of Somanātha *nagara* and of the kingdom of Gujarat under the Caulukya and Caulukya-Vāghelas. The other images of Viśvanātha, according to the record, are those as *Viśvarūpa* (Image of the universe),[30] *Śūnyarūpa* ('Formless' or 'one whose form is the void') and *Lakṣyālakṣya* ('Visible as well as Invisible'). The record then goes on to refer to Viśvanātha also as the Divinity to whom the sailors, with *Rasula* Mahammada as their Prophet (*bodhaka*, i.e. literally, 'one who makes intelligible') were attached (*pratibaddha*).[31] The facile passage from Viśvanātha,[32] representing one name and image of Śiva, to Viśvanātha, representing Divinity in Islam, is parallel to the representation of a mosque

[28] The five great sins (*mahāpātakas*) were: murder of a brāhmaṇa, drinking spirituous liquor, theft (generally of brāhmaṇa's gold), sexual intercourse with wife of preceptor and association with a great sinner. P.V. Kane, *History of Dharmaśāstra (Ancient and Medieval Religious and Civil Law in India)*, vol. 4, Poona, 1953, pp. 15–32.

[29] A Sanskrit text *Śrī Rehamāna-Prāsāda-Lakṣaṇam*, deals with the principles of the construction of what is called *Rehamāna-Prāsāda* ('the temple of Rehamāna', viz., Allah) or *Rehamāna Surālaya*. The text is a part of a larger work called *Vṛkṣārṇava* (*c.* fifteenth century, belonging to the Maru-Gurjara region) and is in the form of a dialogue, with Jaya asking Viśvakarmā questions on the nature, proportions, rhythm, form and types of temples built by the Muslims (mentioned in the text us Mlecchas) under the *Sāttivika-bhāva* or emotion of divine adoration. See R. Nath, 'Rehamāna-Prāsāda: A Chapter on the Muslim Mosque from the Vrksarnava', *Vishveshvaranand Indological Journal*, vol. 15, pt. 2, 1977, pp. 238–44. Nath mentions that M.A. Dhaky who originally published the text also refers to another text, with an independent chapter on *Rehamāna-Prāsāda*, titled *Jaya-pṛcchā* in an article 'Maru-Gurjara-vāstu Śāstramān masjid-nirmāṇa-vidhi', published in Gujarati in the journal *Swadhyaya*, vol. 7.1. See also Romila Thapar, 'Communalism and the Historical Legacy', in *Communalism in India: History. Politics and Culture*, ed. K.N. Panikkar, Delhi, 1991, pp. 17–33.

[30] D.C. Sircar translates *Viśvarūpa* as 'having various forms', ibid., p. 141.

[31] In an earlier reference to the Veraval record, I had committed the serious mistake of taking Viśvanātha to refer to *rasula* Muhammada, the Prophet: Brajadulal Chattopadhyaya, *The Making of Early Medieval India*, Delhi, 1994, p. 197.

[32] Viśvanātha obviously stands as the Sanskritic equivalent of God in Islam.

in the contemporary image of a *dharmasthāna*. Like the sacred site, Divinity too is represented as a locally comprehensible concept.[33]

The Veraval record, along with other evidence such as that relating to the reconstruction of a demolished mosque by an earlier Caulukya ruler Jayasiṃha Siddharāja (1094–1143), has been taken as a remarkable example of religious toleration on the part of the Gujarat rulers.[34] Sectarian and theological conflicts were not unknown in the period, and the reference, in Jayasiṃha Siddharāja's time, to the demolition of a mosque and the killing of eighty Muslims, in which fire-worshippers and infidels are alleged to have been involved,[35] presents one more dimension of the conflict potential in the

[33] There are other significant examples of such attempts to render the image of divinity in a language of common comprehension.

The Batihagarh stone inscription of 1328 from Madhya Pradesh, caused to be written by local ruler Jallāla Khojā, refers to pre-creation creator (*Śṛṣṭikarttā*) of all worlds, 'whose power is subservient to his wish (*icchāśakti*), who is unlimited (*ananta*), who has no beginning and no end (*anādi-nidhanam*), and who is, destitute of quality and colour'. Hira Lal, 'Batihagarh Stone Inscription, Samvat 1385', *EI*, vol. 12, pp. 44–7. The idea of a non-iconic god is similarly conveyed in an extremely interesting inscription in Sanskrit which was composed on the occasion of the construction of a mosque (mentioned in the inscription as *masīti*, the form being identical with that in *Jagaḍū-carita*) by Adil Shah, 'for fostering his own religion' (*sva-dharma-pālanārtham*). Adil Shah, a ruler of Faruqi family of Burhanpur in Khandesh, constructed this mosque in 1590, ten years before Khandesh came to be conquered by Akbar. The creator (*Śṛṣṭikarttā*) is described in this record as imperceptible (*avyakta*), all-pervading (*vyāpaka*), eternal (*nitya*), past all qualities (*guṇātīta*); His essence is mind (*cidātmaka*). He is the cause of what is manifest (*vyktasya kāraṇam*), and He is Himself both manifest and non-manifest (*vyaktāvyakta*, which is comparable to *Lakṣyālakṣya* of the Veraval inscription). The same record conceives God as *guṇagaṇātīta* (beyond all qualities) and *parabrahma*.

The Burhanpur inscription in Sanskrit was obviously commissioned by Adil Shah in addition to the Arabic inscription which too, records the construction of the mosque. The date of the mosque is given in the record in both Vikrama and Śaka eras, and, what is curious, in terms of details of *tithi*, *ghaṭi*, *yoga*, *nakṣatra*, *karaṇa*, *lagna* and so on. Commenting on these details, Hira Lal, editor of the record, adds: 'The astrological details are unique in a Muhammadan mosque and show the religious tendency of the later Faruqi Kings. In Burhanpur much of the belief of the two religions (Hinduism and Islam) got mixed up, traces of which are still conspicuously present there. As an instance may be cited the preaching of the Pirzadas who are Musalmans and who say that God will now become incarnate as Nishkalani.' Hira Lal, 'Burhanpur Sanskrit Inscription of Adil Shah, Samvat 1646', *EI*, vol. 9, 1907–8, Delhi, repr. 1981, pp. 306–10.

[34] Sircar, 'Veraval Inscription'; Desai, 'Muslims in the 13th century Gujarat'.

[35] H.M. Elliot and J. Dowson, *The History of India as told by its own Historians* (*The Muhammadan Period*), vol. 2, Allahabad, repr. n.d., pp. 162–4.

ideological situation of the period.[36] Religious toleration can thus be one possible perspective from which the Veraval record may be considered. At the same time, it must be borne in mind that the record was not composed to demonstrate religious toleration but to record a cluster of events around the building of a mosque, and it would thus seem that one can also interpret the record by trying to understand how the events are represented. The representations, one feels, are attempts at expressing what are 'external' in one's own cultural terms, and evidently, this goes much beyond Sanskritizing non-Sanskrit words alone. They reach out to the more complex planes of religious practice and theological comprehension and present the events within a frame which matches the frame of communication in Sanskrit language, in a Sanskritic and widely recognizable idiom. The Veraval record perhaps in a way contradicts the idea of indigenous insularity alleged by Al-Beruni more than two centuries earlier,[37] and it also brings us back to the problem of attempting to understand varieties of representation. To this we turn now.

[36] A recent publication which provides an overview of the problem, including reference to epigraphical evidence, is Karl-Heinz Golzio, 'Das Problem von Toleranz und Intoleranz in Indischen Religionen anhand Epigraphischer Quellen', in *Frank-Richard Hamm Memorial Volume*, ed. Helmut Eimer, Bonn, 1990, pp. 89–102. I am indebted to Rahul Peter Das for making a copy of this article available to me.

[37] Edward C. Sachau, *Alberuni's India*, vol. 1, London, 1910, pp. 22–3. For an analysis of Al-Beruni's comments see Arvind Sharma, *Studies in 'Alberuni's India'*, Wiesbaden, 1983, Chap. 3. However, pertinent to the present issue is Al-Beruni's following comment, Sachau, vol. I, p. 19: 'They totally differ from us in religion, as we believe in nothing in which they believe, and *vice verse*.' It may be underlined that it is not Veraval record alone which is available to contradict this essentialism.

CHAPTER 4

Conclusion

If the historical sources cited earlier are seen to contain representations of communities which may have been considered as 'others' by those who created these sources, then, in undertaking to examine them, we may as well remind ourselves that we too stand in a relation of otherness to these other two categories of the 'other'. In other words, the present field of study is one in what the agencies concerned—the represented, the representer and the interpreter(s) of representations—are multiple, and any presumptive, unilineal explanation of the sources pertaining to the field would be an inadequate recognition of how complex the nuances of perception and representation may have been. The explanations which are presently available appear to be largely unilineal and appear to be based on the predetermined device of essentializing two communities:[1] Hindu and Muslim. This predetermined essentialization in the historiography of the early medieval period in which the Muslims are present has sometimes been forcefully questioned, but, by and large, the implicit recognition of essential difference between two 'homogeneous' communities and culture is what continues to

[1] The term 'essentialization' is derived from Peter van der Veer, '"The Foreign Hand": Orientalist Discourse in Sociology and Communalism', in *Orientalism and the Postcolonial Predicament: Perspectives on South Asia*, ed. Carol A. Breckenridge and Peter van der Veer, Philadelphia, 1993, pp. 23–44. Although van der Veer believes in the historical existence of essentializing features of Hindu (perhaps elite) discourses about the Muslim 'other' and of Muslim discourses about the Hindu 'other', our evidence seems to suggest that there may not have existed an essential, elite discourse about specifically Muslims as 'others' but that Muslims, when required, could be absorbed in existing categories. Second, the elite discourse itself was not fixed in relation to 'others' in all contexts.

colour how, from a distance, we ourselves perceive and represent this period.[2] Starting from the essential difference of two well-formed communities in ethnic and cultural terms, the historiographical positions which follow range from the underscoring of irreconcilable hostility[3] to religious toleration and synthesis.[4] Explanations in material terms, seeking to attribute invasions and attendant atrocities to political and economic expediencies are also available.[5]

One of the strongest statements of irreconcilable hostility, which is matched only by characterizing Indian reaction to ethnic traits of invading Turks of the later twelfth century in terms of xenophobia,[6] comes from the editors of the Vilasa Grant cited:

[2] For a critique see Romila Thapar, 'Imagined Religious Communities? Ancient History and the Modern Search for a Hindu Identity', in *Interpreting Early India*, ed. R. Thapar, Delhi, 1992.

[3] A recent statement of this is Sheldon Pollock, 'Ramayana and Political Imagination in India'.

[4] See the important work of Tara Chand, *Influence of Islam on Indian Culture*, Allahabad, 1976.

[5] 'Economic and imperialistic considerations rather than religious zeal' were underlined as the 'inspiring motive' in such writings as those of Mohammad Habib. See K.A. Nizami, ed., *Politics and Society during the Early Medieval Period: Collected Works of Professor Mohammad Habib*, vol. 2, Delhi, 1981, Introduction. See also K.M. Ashraf, *Life and Conditions of the People of Hindustan*, 3rd edn., Delhi, 1988, pp. 40–6.

[6] This comes from Sheldon Pollock who believes that the description of the Ghurid ambassador to the court of Pṛthvīrāja Cāhamāna 'provides almost a paradigm of xenophobic differentiation'. Sheldon Pollock, 'Ramayana and Political Imagination in India', *The Journal of Asian Studies*, vol. 53, no. 2, 1993, p. 276. However, differentiation in terms of behavioural and other traits between communities in India was nothing new. Note, for example, the following references, in *Pādaltāḍitaka*, a *bhāṇa* or monologue play, assigned to the Gupta period: (1) 'Aha, this is the character of a *diṇḍi*. The *diṇḍis* are not very different from the monkeys, O, what does he then find lovable in the *diṇḍis*?; (2) 'Here is a man with the face of a he-goat, whose loins are covered with a piece of cloth, and whose shoulders are full of thick hairs. (Besides) he comes biting a radish. If he is not a Dāśeraka then he must be a devil'; (3) 'What merit has he discovered in this (slave) maid Barbarikā . . . ? Moreover, this Barbarī, the veritable goddess of darkness with whiteness in the teeth and eyes only, appears like night with a very strip of the crescent moon. But this is not strange. For the men of Surāṣṭra and the monkeys are all of the same class'; (4) '. . . who will listen to the Yavana courtesans words which are like the chattering of a monkey, full of shrill sounds and of indistinguishable consonants and which are interspersed with the (occasional) display of the forefingers?' M. Ghosh, *Glimpses of Sexual Life in Nanda-Maurya India*, translation of the *Cuturbhāṇī* with a critical edition of the text, Calcutta, 1976, pp. 133, 135, 155, 157; G.M. Schokker, *The Pādatāḍitaka of Śyāmilaka*, pt. I, The Hague, 1966; G.H. Schokker and P.J. Worseley, *The Pādatāḍitaka of Śyāmilaka*, pt. 2, Dordrect, 1976.

Unlike other conquerors of India, the Musalmans were not satisfied with the acquisition of mere political power. They descended on the Deccan not as mere conquerors in search of new countries but as crusading warriors to spread the true faith in the land of the infidels. To stamp out heathenism and gather all the people within the fold of Islam, they prohibited, as stated in the inscription, the public exercise of Hindu religion, and subjected its followers to inhuman tyranny. . . . [U]nable to bear the grinding tyranny of the Musalmans, which was set on foot to wipe out their race, religion and culture, the Andhras as a people joined together and rose up in revolt. . . . It was the first national movement in Indian history; and the Andhras showed to the rest of India how a people could, by their united effort, expel the enemy and regain their lost freedom.[7]

This construction of the representation available in Vilasa grant may have made the editors of the grant somewhat uncomfortable if they had tried to reconcile it with the reference they themselves make to the collaboration between the Kakatiyas (who were overthrown by the Muslims who, in turn, were overthrown in Andhra by Prola Nāyaka) and the Muslim forces and their combined intervention in the Pāṇḍya kingdom in order 'to restore Sundara Pāṇḍya to the ancestral throne'.[8] In fact, within about fifty years from the date of the Vilasa grant, Lakṣmaṇa Paṇḍita, associated with the court of Vijayanagara, was accusing, in his *Vaidya-rājavallabham,* the Velama king of Telingana of defiant attitude and pride, 'on account of the accession of strength by his alliance with the Yavanas'. Further, Visveśvara, associated with the Velamas, mentioned with pride in his introduction to the *Camatkāracandrikā,* 'the amity that prevailed between his patron and the Pārasīka-*nṛpati*'.[9] The point is that there could be various empirical realities in political relations between Yavana and non-Yavana powers, and there could be various representations too. Historical reconstruction has to contend with

---

Similarly, the character of Grāharipu, ruler of Saurāṣṭradeśa and of Ābhīra origin, as depicted in *Dvyāśraya-mahākāvya* of Hemacandra is an example of deliberate differentiation, to highlight the model character of Mūlarāja, the Caulukya ruler. Grāharipu is described as a cruel tyrant, anti-religious, killer of pilgrims, and he is one 'who causes calamities, plunders people and destroys forts and important places', Chandra Prabha, *Historical Mahākāvyas in Sanskrit (Elevent to Fifteenth Century* AD), Delhi, 1976, pp. 184–6. Note also the manner in which Chittukka, described as an *asura,* is referred to in the Vadavali plates of Śilāhāra king Aparāditya I; V.V. Mirashi, *Inscriptions of the Śilāhāras,* Corpus Inscriptionum Indicarum, vol. 6, Delhi, 1977, pp. 120–7.

[7] N. Venkataramanayya and M. Somasekhara Sharma, 'Vilasa Grant of Prolaya Nayaka', EI, vol. 32, 1957–8, Delhi, repr. 1987, pp. 248–9.

[8] Ibid., p. 247.

[9] Both sources are cited by N. Venkataramanayya (one of the editors of the Vilasa Grant): 'Kaleśvaram Inscription of Devaraya I, Śaka 1319, *EI*, vol. 36, Delhi, repr. 1987, pp. 199–202.

these various representations. If one takes the Vilasa grant or the *Madhurā-vijaya* of Gaṅgādevī, offering graphic accounts of devastations caused by Muslim rule, for constructing empirical reality and for understanding past attitude in essentialist terms, then one should simultaneously be turning to the task of reconciling them with the images of the Sultanate and the Mughal rule and the attitude reflected in such sources of these periods as the Palam Baoli inscription and the *Bhānucandra-carita*.

The perspectives of synthesis or of political expediency, which in a way seek to replace the essentialist approach, would be found somewhat inadequate in accommodating the very distinctive features of the ideological systems that came into contact with one another in this historical phase. These distinctive features, in the context of the reality of historical events, differentially informed the representation of the same empirical reality—one could thus have different versions of the same text. And this was so, despite the fact (as seen, for example, in the Kotla-Mubarakpur inscription of the early sixteenth century) that synthesis and incorporation were processes that can be located in different regions of medieval India.[10] That the same event, or cluster of events, could be presented in different ways is clear, among our sources, in the Veraval record, in the variations between the Sanskrit text and the Arabic text. The Sanskrit text presents the features connected with the construction of the mosque, its rituals and its maintenance—features outside its linguistic and conceptual parameters—in terms of its own vocabulary and concepts, or by attempts at Sanskritization; the Arabic text simply presents the events and features, within its own linguistic and ideological parameters. The ideological parameters are not absent even when political-economic expediency seems to explain events with great clarity; however, at the same time, ideological parameters do not represent permanently bounded space either.

If the evidence from Sanskrit sources presented earlier is seen not as photocopy of empirical reality but as representation within the broad cultural-ideological parameters of early Indian society, then we may perhaps understand the curiously contradictory images present in them in terms of the brahmanical ambivalence of inclusivity and exclusivity, or, to put it

[10] Local, ground-level realities, which are different from essentialist generalizations, explain not only commonness in language and living styles, but significant coming together in the practice of religion—particularly at the non-elite level—as well. See Susan Bayly, *Saints, Goddesses and Kings: Muslims and Christians in South Indian Society 1700–1900*, Delhi, Indian edn., 1992, 1.3; R. Eaton, *Bengal and the Islamic Frontier*, pp. 77–82, 275–81. Also Romila Thapar, 'The Tyranny of Labels', 9th Annual Zakir Hussain Memorial Lecture, *Social Scientist* 280-81, vol. 24, nos. 9–10, 1997, pp. 3–23.

differently, in terms of legitimation and, at the same time, of the device of distancing.

The legitimation of political authority in terms of brahmanical discourse is abundantly documented in early medieval India.[11] Brahmanical discourse, it must be qualified, was not limited to the society as defined solely by *dharmaśāstric* Brahmanism. In different forms, at the core of legitimation lay the notion of authority extending to the temporal power through its source, the spiritual domain or the domain of transcendence. What the brahmanical discourse did not make explicit was the absolute dependence of the spiritual authority on support from the temporal domain and, therefore, the essential urge to legitimize. The modes of legitimation underwent significant changes over time, and the Sanskrit sources of the early medieval period show us that current motifs could be combined with new elements, by suitably transforming such elements to adjust with recognizable cultural conventions. *Suratrāṇa,* transformed from Sultan, would be an example of this. Although origin myths and genealogies as major modes of legitimation are not seen in use in relation to rulers of Delhi, one gets occasional evidence, as in the case of the Kotihar inscription, dated 1369, of tracing the descent of a Sultan, from the epic lineage of the Pāṇḍavas.[12] The deployment of current motifs is seen in abundance in the Palam Baoli inscription of the thirteenth century, and even if origin myths and genealogies do not seem to characterize legitimation of Muslim rule, there is nevertheless evidence of attempt to structure the portrayal of a ruler along lines which a *Carita* text would generally follow. Although *Bhānucandra-carita,* cited earlier, was written as a biography of the Jaina monk Bhānucandra and his disciple, the biographer, Siddhicandra, the text is also an excellent example of what may be called reciprocal legitimation: the spiritual domain here is sought to be legitimized as an instrument for the enhancement of the authority of emperors Akbar and Jahangir. Throughout the text the personalities of the Jaina teachers are projected by highlighting their associations with Akbar and Jahangir as well as with Akbar's *saciva, Sāhi-Saciva-Śekha-Ābala-Fajala* (Abul Fazl).[13] Akbar is represented as having his bad karma annihilated through his association with them, and in fact, he became the protector of the six philosophies in the same manner as a cowherd protects his herd of animals (*ṣaḍdarśana-paśugrāma-gopāla-iva-pālayan*). Had *Jahāṅgira-Śāha-Carita* which Rudrakavi, the author of *Rāṣṭrauḍha-vaṃśa-mahākāvya*[14] wrote at the instance of his patron Pratāpa

[11] For bibliographical references see my essay 'Political Processes and Structure of Polity in Early Medieval India', in *The Making of Early Medieval India,* Chap. 8.

[12] B.K. Kaul Deambi, *Corpus of Śāradā Inscriptions of Kashmir,* Delhi, 1982, pp. 113–18.

[13] *Bhānucandra-carita,* 1.4.

[14] See Introduction to *Rāṣṭrauḍha-vaṃśa-mahākāvya.*

Śāha, been published in detail, it could make an interesting comparison, in terms of its narrative structure, with *Rāṣṭrauḍha-vaṃśa-mahākāvya*.

The existence of the ruler of Delhi, and of others, who figure within the narrative structures of the Sanskrit texts of the medieval period regularly is not considered as incompatible with the *Rāmarājya* such as that of the local kingdom of the Chandrawat rulers of Mandasor (Madhya Pradesh) in the period of Akbar. In the *Rāṣṭrauḍha-vaṃśa-mahākāvya* too, Nārāyaṇa Śāha, the Bagula ruler of Mayūragiri, could be described as *Śrīmad-akhila-bhūpāla-mauli-mukuṭa-lalāma-mālā-mārīci-vīci-cumbita-caraṇa-saroja-Mayūragiri-kesari* (briefly, 'the lion of Mayūragiri whose lotus-like feet have been kissed by the crowns of all rulers'). The title of one *sarga* (19th) in the *Rāṣṭrauḍha-vaṃśa-mahākāvya* is *Śāha-Murāda-samāgama-kautuka*; it deals with Mughal expedition to Gujarat and the Deccan in which the support of the Bagula ruler was sought by Akbar. The idea of getting a text like *Jahāṅgira-Śāha-Carita* written by his resident poet, by Pratāpa Śāha, mentioned as a Zamindar by Jahangir in his Memoirs,[15] reveals a strategy of political legitimation, in which the ruler of Delhi had to be the central figure. In fact, even in the Vilasa grant of Prola, the Delhi Sultan who brought calamity to Andhradeśa, is seen as representing a sequal to Paraśurāma,[16] 'in his role as the destroyer of the kṣatriyas; the motif which is used is thus not out of line with the general repertoire of motifs for representation.

It may be noted that the graphic detail of calamity which follows the Muslim occupation of a kingdom, be it Andhra or Madurai, is a flash-back which brings into bright relief the present when the defeat of the Turuṣka or the Yavana has been achieved. When the Yavana is not ruler, he fits into a category for which the device of legitimation becomes inappropriate. Then the representation of the Yavana or Mleccha is that of an excluded group. It has been suggested in a recent study that 'under no circumstances and during no period were ethnicity or religious factors which determined [*sic*] the existence of Mlecchas and outsiders in Indian society'.[17] The idea of exclusion from the recognized social structure, though sometimes done in terms of a 'sacerdotal conception of Āryāvarta', with time came to derive more from the brahmanical ideology of *Varṇāśrama dharma;* any group which is seen as outside of or opposed to it could be considered as Mleccha. There was an element of timelessness in this perception; '. . . the perpetual existence of Mlecchas as a theoretical category co-existed easily

[15] See *The Tuzuk-i-Jahangīrī*, tr. A. Rogers, ed. H. Beveridge, 2nd edn., Delhi, 1968, vol. I, pp. 396, 411.

[16] Venkataramanayya and Somasekhara Sharma, 'Vilasa Grant', pp. 260–1.

[17] Aloka Parashar, *Mlecchas in Early India: A Study in Attitude Towards Outsiders upto* AD *600*, Delhi, 1991, p. 20.

with conscious attempts made by the brāhmaṇas to use it as a designation for particular groups sparingly, and with a flexibility'.[18] Not being in conformity with *Varṇāśrama dharma* defined the behaviour pattern of the Mleccha, be the Mleccha a *vyādha* or hunter of the Vindhya forest, or a Yavana or Turuṣka of the early medieval/medieval period. The Mlecchas were the 'dirt of mankind' (*manuṣāṇam malaṃ Mlecchāḥ*); the calamity wrought by the Mleccha could be redeemed only with the advent of Kalki. Note the following description in the *Yuga-Purāṇa:* 'Then that red-eyed and red-attired clever Mleccha king Āmlāta will destroy the *varṇas;* he will totally upset the established order'.[19]

The dark foreboding that the entire universe will be Mleccha, inactive, sacrificeless (*yajñavarjitam*); joyless, and bereft of festivities (*anutsavam*) is present in the *Mahābhārata;*[20] as Mleccha dharma is in total opposition to real *dharma,* the Kali age stands for vice, violence, hatred, falsehood, lack of virtue in women, neglect in the authority of the *Smṛti* and in the study of the Veda. The Purāṇic description of Yavana rule as an inevitability of the future also includes these grim features:

There will be Yavanas here for reasons of *dharma, artha* and *kāma.* They will not be properly anointed kings and will follow evil customs (*yugadoṣa-durācāraḥ*). Massacring women and children, and killing one another, kings will enjoy the earth at the end of the Kali Age. . . . [T]he population will perish (*viparyayeṇa vartante kṣayameṣyanti vai prajāh*).[21]

The apprehension of the fall of the social order is so acute that the *Mārkaṇḍeya Purāṇa* makes the clear pronouncement that the four varṇas 'must be safeguarded according to their respective rules of righteousness, and dāsas, mlecchas and others who live in wickedness must be slain'.[22]

The element of timelessness which made it possible for the category of Mleccha/Yavana to reach out to and accommodate the Tājikas and the Turuṣkas[23] was also the element which defined the attributes, and the

[18] Ibid., p. 273.

[19] Ibid., p. 121.

[20] Ibid., p. 123.

[21] Ibid., p. 122.

[22] Ibid., p. 121.

[23] It is not xenophobia against particular social groups or the concrete historical reality of xenophobia which can be constructed out of the textual perception of the Mleccha; it would be impossible, if one assumes the inevitability of the correspondence of this perception to actual historical process, to analyse either integration or juxtaposition of diverse communities within a territorially defined society. Yet, the notion of exclusion could be strong and could lead, as in the case of Al-Beruni, well-versed in theoretical literature, to powerful articulation about what it meant to be a foreigner: '. . . all their

representation, of the new entrants to the category. If the Yavanas of earlier times destroyed dharma and ruined the population, the new Yavanas too had the same quality of destruction. And destruction did not imply political subjugation alone; it had to mean the destruction of the social order as well—to make space for the rejuvenation of that particular social order, informed by the use of the motifs that belong to the brahmanical discourse,[24] in greater splendour than before.

It has been suggested recently that despite the fixity of the notion of *Varṇāśrama dharma,* the assimilation of the Mlecchas into the social order defined by it was an ongoing process.[25] This was indeed a major historical process in the evolution of Indian social structure, but it does not mean that the Mleccha category disappeared altogether or that the Mlecchas necessarily needed to be incorporated through the single entry gate of *Varṇāśrama dharma.* The options for representation open then were either to legitimize the Mlecchas who remained Mlecchas, as a contingent strategy, in terms of motifs which could be considered appropriate legitimizing motifs, or to relate them with what was perceived as the destruction of social order.[26]

In looking for an explanation of the contradiction which seems to characterize the representations of the Muslims in the Sanskrit sources, one is not denying the empirical reality of invasions and of religious persecution. But empirical reality is also a matter of representation; the problem here is that many a time historians tend to 'use historical narrations almost exclusively as unstructured, uninterpretive mines of factual information' and are usually 'content to ask what information the source provides that

---

fanaticism is directed against those who do not belong to them—*against all foreigners* [emphasis mine]. They call them *mlechchha,* i.e. impure, and forbid having any connection with them . . . in all manners and usages they differ from us to such a degree as to frighten their children with us, with our dress, and our ways and customs, and as to declare us to be devil's breed and our doings as the very opposite of all that is good and proper.' Edward C. Sachau, *Alberuni's India,* vol. I, London, 1910, pp. 19–20. One should note the remarkable similarity between Mleccha of the texts and Al-Beruni's 'self'-perception as a Mleccha. Al-Beruni was obviously not referring to either the Mlecchas within Indian society or the Mlecchas of history.

[24] See the contents of the Vilasa grant from Andhra cited in detail earlier.

[25] Parashar, *Mlecchas,* Chap. 8.

[26] With reference to the representation of the Muslims as destroyers of the social order in the Vilasa grant, Cynthia Talbot has recently commented: 'The depiction of Muslim behaviour in the Vilasa Grant is formulaic . . . and follows a pattern expected of foreign groups in the Brāhmaṇical tradition', 'Inscribing the Other, Inscribing the Self: Hindu-Muslim Identities in Pie-Colonial India', *Comparative Studies in Society and History,* vol. 37, 1995, pp. 4, 692–722. I have, however, been trying to show that there is more than one pattern in the brahmanic tradition.

can be useful for solving his own problems'.[27] I have been trying to argue that in the process of historical reconstruction we tend to convert a single representation into an absolute empirical reality, without even instituting comparisons. This, one must need underline, is as possible a slip in other sources as it is in the case of Sanskrit sources.

The references to groups which would constitute the category Muslim, and impressions of them embedded in the Sanskrit sources that we have been dealing with, can now be given a final review. It is clear that the sources do not project the image of the Muslims as an undifferentiated 'other'. There were three choices available to the composers of the written documents concerning the manner in which the Muslims could be referred to: to mention them as *Musalamānas*; in terms of their different ethnic and spatial origins; by using one or more generic terms. The fact that the last two alternatives were chosen should be considered significant. One point of significance is that the perception of the diverse Muslim communities was in terms of their diverse origins. When generic terms were used, they were generally, but not invariably, used to highlight difference; the difference, crucial to representation, was perceived in terms of closeness to or distance from the ideal moral order: adherence to or protection of the moral order would entitle a Muslim to representation in terms which would apply to any similar adherent to the moral order. Violence to this moral order in the form of destruction of temples and idols, appropriation of *agrahāras* and eating of beef would bring up the image of the terrible other.[28] To talk of all-pervading xenophobia is therefore absurd. It should be noted that the construction of

[27] Marilyn Robinson Waldman, 'Toward a Mode of Criticism for Premodern Islamicate Historical Narratives', in *Toward a Theory of Historical Narrative: A Case Study in Perso-Islamicate Historiography*, ed. M.R. Waldman, Columbus, 1980, pp. 3–4, Chap. 1.

[28] In fact, this is precisely why king Harsa of Kashmir (1089–1102) who was notorious for destruction of temples and images was described as a Turuṣka. Note the following details about this king, as they appear in the *Rājataranginị:*

'Then the greedy-minded [king] plundered from all temples the wonderful treasures which former kings had bestowed there. In order to get hold of the statues of gods, too, when the treasures [of the temples] had been carried off, he appointed Udayaraja "prefect for the overthrow of divine images" (*devotpatana—nāyaka*). In order to defile the statues of gods he had excrements and wine poured over their faces by naked mendicants whose noses, feet and hands had rotted away. Divine images made of gold, silver, and other [materials] rolled about even on the roads, which were covered with night soil, as [if they were] logs of wood. . . . There was not one temple in a village, town or in the city which was not despoiled of its images by that Turuṣka king Harsa', *Rājataranginị,*VII, 1090–5. [M.A. Stein, *Kalhaṇa's Rājataranginị: A Chronicle of the Kings of Kashmir*, Delhi, repr. 1979, pt. 1.]

the other is made neither in religious nor in territorial terms; in other words, although the term dharma is used in the sense of religion, the Muslims are not projected as a community practising a religion which is the antithesis of recognized religious practices. The historical context of the destruction of a mosque in Cambay during the reign of Caulukya Jayasiṃha Siddharāja is unknown and is unlikely to have been religious. Similarly, the Muslim communities are not projected as outsiders territorially, as the notion of territorial outsider in a political sense does not seem compatible with early cosmological/geographical concepts.

The Muslim other, when the generic category of Mleccha, Yavana or Turuṣka is invoked to refer to this other, is therefore a social outsider whose moral order would be considered incompatible with the order defined by *Varṇdharma*. This otherness in Indian society is not new; communities within India, and from outside, had been representing this otherness for centuries. The brahmanical discourse of society, informed by this notion of otherness, was therefore always marked by a keen apprehension about the other and of the collapse of the social order through the instrumentality of the other. At the same time, otherness in society was historical and could be a source of conflict. Conflict was not specific to the political plane alone; it also involved destruction of the symbols of moral order and culture. Conflict, which could be both inter-community and intra-community was, however, one pattern in the totality of social existence. A situation of unmitigated hostility and conflict through centuries would not have produced the kind of evidence that we have cited above.

To convert what we have described as the notion of the other in the brahmanical discourse, or for that matter in Al-Beruni, into a major disjunction in Indian history is to ignore major processes of change in Indian society, and, in particular, such processes as were associated with the shaping of regional societies and cultural patterns. Perhaps a better idea, than what we have now, of how society and culture in medieval India developed, may be gained by heuristically comparing the stereotype of a major disjunction projected in a centralized historiographical discourse with the trajectories and patterns of historical movements in regional societies. Perhaps it is only then that we can disabuse ourselves of our derived wisdoms about inter-community relations in Indian history.

APPENDIX 1

Pattern of the occurrence of terms referring to Muslims in Epigraphic and Literary Texts

Date	*Source*	*Term used*	*Reference*
I. EIGHTH TO TENTH CENTURIES			
22 June 736	Kavi plates (Gujarat) of Jayabhaṭa	*Tājika*	*CII*, 4, pt. I, 96–102.
9 October 736	Prince of Wales Museum plates of Jayabhaṭa	*Tājika*	Ibid., 102–9.
Second half of eighth century	Hund, Attock district Pakistan	*Turuṣka*	*EI*, 38, 94–8.
795	Inscription of Pratīhāra Vatsarāja (povenance unknown)	*Mleccha* *Tājika*	*EI*, 41, 94–7.
Ninth century	Gwalior inscription of Bhoja (MP)	*Mleccha*, *Turuṣka*	*EI*, 18, 99–114.
926	Chinchani (Konkan, Mahārashtra) plates of Rāṣṭrakūṭa Indra III	*Tājika*	*EI*, 32, 45–54.

* This is not a comprehensive list, but is intended primarily to give an impression of spatial and chronological distribution of relevant terms. It may be considered as fairly representative. For a pioneering effort to compile references from inscriptions see R.S. Avasthy and A. Ghosh, 'References to Muhammedans in Sanskrit Inscriptions in Northern India—AD 730 to 1320', *Journal of Indian History*, vol. 15, 1936, pp. 161–84; vol. 16, 1937–8, pp. 24–6.

Date	Source	Term used	Reference
Middle of tenth century	Chinchani plates of Rāṣṭrakūṭa Kṛṣṇa II	*Tājika, Pārasīka*	*EI*, 32, 55–60.
II. ELEVENTH TO TWELFTH CENTURIES			
Middle of the eleventh century	Udaipur (Malwa, MP) inscription of Paramara Bhoja	*Turuṣka*	*EI*, 1, 223–8.
1059	Panjim (Goa) plates of Kadamba Jayakeśi I	*Tājiya-vaṃśa*	G.M. Moraes, *Kadamba-kula*.
1079	Amoda (Bilaspur, MP) inscription of Ratanpur Kalacuri Pṛthvīdeva I	*Turuṣka*	*CII*, 4, pt. 2. 404–5.
1095	Kharepatan (Ratnagiri, Mahārashtra) inscription of Śilāhāra Anantadeva	*Yavana*	*CII*, 6, 115–20.
Close of eleventh and beginning of twelfth century	Kashmir	*Turuṣka*, used as an appellation of King Harṣa of Kashmir	*Rājataraṅgiṇi* VII, 1095.
1109	Rahan (Etawah, UP) inscription of Gāhaḍavāla Madanapāla and Govindacandra	*Hammīra*	*IA*, 18 (1889), 14–19.
c.1110	Benares, UP	*Hammīravira*	*Kṛiyakalpataru*[1]
Close of the eleventh century	Chidambaram inscription of Kulottuṅga Cola I	*Pārasī*	*EI*, 5, 104.
Early twelfth century	Sarnath inscription of Gāhaḍavāla Govindacandra's wife Kumarādevī	*Turuṣka*, described as *duṣṭa*	*EI*, 9, 324, 327.
Early twelfth century	Mahoba (UP) inscription of Candella Jayavarman	*Hamvīra*, described as *bhuvanātibhāra* and *atibala*	*EI*, 1, 217–22.
1127	Vadavali (Thane, Mahārashtra) inscription of Śilāhāra Aparāditya I	*Mleccha*	*CII*, 6,120–7.

[1] K.V. Rangaswami Aiyangar, ed., *Kṛtyakalpataru of Bhaṭṭa Lakṣmīdhara*, vol. 5, *Dānakāṇḍa*, Baroda, 1941, pp. 48, 53.

Date	*Source*	*Term used*	*Reference*
1164	Delhi-Siwalik Pillar inscription of Cāhamāna Vīsaladeva	*Mleccha*	*IA*, 19, 215–19.
1167	Hansi (Haryana) stone inscription of Cāhamāna Pṛthvīrāja II	*Hammīra-vīra*, mentioned as *Vasumatī-śalya*	*IA*, 41, 17–21.
1167	Jabalpur (MP) inscription of Kalacuri Jayasiṃha	*Turuṣka*	*CII*, 4, pt. I, 324–31.
1175	Benares College Plate of Jayaccandra	*Hamvīra*	*IA*, 18, 129–34.
1180–1	Kumbhi Plates of Kalacuri Vijayasiṃha	*Turuṣka*	*CII*, 4, pt. 2, 649.
1191	Etawah Fort inscription, UP	*Gori, Turaka*	P. Prasad, 43–5.
*c.*1190–2	Ajmer, Rajasthan	*Mleccha, Mātaṅga. Gorī*	*Pṛthvīrāja-vijaya.*[2]
1197	Machchlisar, Jaunpur, inscription of the Gāhaḍavālas	*Hammīra*	P. Prasad, 58–70.
Close of the twelfth century	Jhansi (UP) stone inscription of Sallakṣaṇasiṃha	*Yavana*	*EI*, 1, 214–17.
Close of the twelfth century	Etawah, UP	*Mleccha*	P. Prasad, 92–3.
1206	Kadi (Gujarat) Plates of Bhīmadeva II	*adhirāja* of *Garjaṇaka*, described as *durjaya*	*IA*, 6, 194–5.
1223			Ibid., 197.
1226		*Mleccha*	Ibid., 199.
1230, 1231		*Garjjaṇaka*	Ibid., 200–4.
1238		*Mleccha, Garjjaṇaka*	Ibid., 205.
1239		*Mleccha*	Ibid., 207.
1242		*Garjjaṇaka*	Ibid., 208.

[2] Cited in Chandra Prabha, *Historical Mahākāvyas in Sanskrit (Eleventh to Fifteenth Century* AD), Delhi, 1976, Chap. 4; Sheldon Pollock, 'Ramayana and Political Imagination in India', *The Journal of Asian Studies*, vol. 53, no. 2, 1993, pp. 273–6.

Date	Source	Term used	Reference
Twelfth-thirteenth centuries	Badaun (UP) Stone inscription of Rāṣṭrakūṭa Lakhanapala	*Hambīra*	*EI*, 1, 61–6.
III. THIRTEENTH TO FOURTEENTH CENTURIES			
1253	Dabhoi (Gujarat) inscription of Vāghela Vīsaladeva	*Turuṣka, Mleccha*	*EI*, 1, 20–32.
1261	Ajayagadh inscription of Candella Trailokyavarman	*Turuṣka*	*EI*, 1, 325–30.
1262	Sundha Hill (west Rajasthan) inscription of Cācigadeva	*Turuṣka*	*EI*, 9, 72, 77.
1264	Veraval inscription of the time of Vāghela Arjunadeva	*Musalamāna*	*EI*, 34, 149.
1276	Palam (Delhi) inscription of the time of Ghiyasuddin Balban	*Śaka*	P. Prasad, 3–15.
1325	Mallavaram (Nellore) inscription of Vema	*Mleccha, Yavana*	*Nellore District Inscriptions*, 3, Ongole 73.
1327	Naraina, Delhi	*Śaka*	P. Prasad, 22–7.
1328	Sarban, Delhi	*Mleccha, Turuṣka*	Ibid., 27–31.
1328	Batihagarh (MP) stone inscription of Jallāla Khojā	Sultān Mahmud of Delhi described as *Śākendra*	*EI*, 12, 44–7.
*c.*1330	Vilasa (Pithapuram, East Godavari district) grant of Prolaya Nāyaka	*Yavana, Turuṣka, Pārasīka*	*EI*, 32, 239–68.
Second half of fourteenth century?	Gujarat?	*Garjaṇeśa, Mudgala*	*Jagaḍū-carita*, 6.65; 6.127; 7.35.
1385, 1403	Annavarappadu (West Godavari district, Andhra Pradesh) inscription of Vema of Paṇṭanāḍu	*Yavana*	*EI*, 36, 167ff.

Date	*Source*	*Term used*	*Reference*
IV. FIFTEENTH TO SEVENTEENTH CENTURIES			
1424	Lalitpur Stone inscription, UP	*Gaurī-Kula*	P. Prasad, 183–99.
1596	Gujarat	*Yavana* with reference to *Allāvadina* and others (3.11:3.37; 3.39); *Turuṣka* with reference to soldiers of *Dillīśvara* (3.33); *Mleccha* with reference to a *bhūpati* or *bhūmipati* (4.6); *Mugila* with reference to Mughal Humayun (6.34); *Paṭhaṇa* (7.35); *pātriśāha* (6.29) and *Sulatāna* (6.28).	*Rāṣṭraudha-vaṃśa-mahākāvya.*
1607	Rampura, Mandasaur district, MP	*Mleccha, Yavana, Śaka, Turati*[3]	*EI*, 36, 121–30

[3] Sadhu Ram, editor of the record, suggests that Turbat being the name of a tribe in Khurasan. Turati may be a corruption of this Khurasani tribal name.

APPENDIX 2

Anachronism of Political Imagination

In a highly misleading essay, cited in Chapter 1 of our text, Sheldon Pollock has recently attempted[1] to prove that between the eleventh (but more particularly the twelfth) and the fourteenth centuries, considered by him to be a 'particular historical juncture', 'a *Rāmāyaṇa* imagery came more centrally and dramatically to inhabit a public political space, as opposed to simply a literary space' (262).[2] The specific *Rāmāyaṇa* imagery that Pollock is referring to is that of Rāma as the destroyer of *rākṣasa* Rāvaṇa, Rāvaṇa of this imagery being the metaphor of the demoniac Turuṣkas whose political power was being established in India on a firm basis between the eleventh and the fourteenth centuries. Pollock thinks that the 'adoption of the *Rāmāyaṇa*'—adoption seemingly connoting a deliberate, well thought-out act—'to process the events of the eleventh to fourteenth centuries suggests a complex interplay of culture and political power' (288). Although Pollock talks about the 'reappropriation of this imaginary in contemporary India' (288), the use of the term 'reappropriation' is not really in accord with his thesis which is that '. . . the *Rāmāyaṇa* has served for thousand years as a code in which protocommunalist relations could be activated and theocratic legitimation could be rendered' (288). In other words, after its 'adoption' the *Rāmāyaṇa* did not need to be reappropriated, its adoption having determined, once for all, the direction of inter-community relations in India.

[1] Sheldon Pollock, 'Ramayana and Political Imagination in India', *The Journal of Asian Studies*, vol. 53, no. 2, 1993, pp. 261–97.

[2] Numerical figures within brackets refer to page numbers in Pollock's essay.

Pollock's article was published in the aftermath of the demolition of the Babri mosque and the most virulent form of communal rioting which swept across the entire country preceding and following the event. Pollock begins his essay with a reference to the events of the early nineties, to the 'symbolic nexus' between 'occasion' and 'excuse', and, in my understanding without any relevance whatsoever to the possibility of a particular political party becoming 'the next ruling party of the country' (261). Pollock has used the expressions 'historicist interventionism' (288) and 'critical interventionism' (289) in probing into the question 'of the relationship of historical knowledge and cultural critique', and seems to regard 'scientization' of an historical problem as 'misdirected interventionism' (289):

It is not easy, then, to sustain a claim for literary-critical or historiographical intervention in the face of problems that are not, in fact, literary-critical or historiographical but something else, whether postcolonial nativism, religious identity crises, political mobilization, or a new phenomenon that awaits categorization. One would think that our target should be the 'denunciation-text' rather than the object-text to which the former refers by what are often most tenuous representations (292).

Pollock strongly feels that 'Ayodhyā would hardly have assumed the dimensions of the present problem, were it not for scientized historicality itself (objectified in such texts as the archaeological reports and colonial gazetteers constantly cited by the parties to the dispute) and the pursuit of origins it delusively inspires' (292). And yet, it is not only that there is no 'denunciation-text' in Pollock's thesis but, on the other hand, while apparently 'abandoning the dangerous and chimerical quest for the originary in history' (292), Pollock does in reality take up the question of origins, 'the quest for the originary' in his case being the text of the *Rāmāyaṇa* becoming 'adopted' for 'encoding the paired forces of xenophobia and theocracy' (293). Pollock has not clarified how 'through analysis of the construction and function of such a meaning system' (293) one can, as he claims it can be done, begin to neutralize the forces of xenophobia and theocracy; but from the way he has projected the historical transformation of the text of the *Rāmāyaṇa* as the 'specific symbolic work' of xenophobia and theocracy; one can go about deriving legitimacy for both from his special brand of pursuit of origins.

II

Pollock suggests, and this is a suggestion which has emanated from other authors too, that the text of the *Rāmāyaṇa* has been the most effective text in South Asia for the production of 'an idiom or vocabulary for political imagination' (262) and that 'there is a long history to the relationship between

Rāmāyaṇa and political symbology' (262). However, in the first thousand years of its existence, *the Rāmāyaṇa* affected the political imagination of India only superficially; 'but something very different happens early in the next millennium'; '. . . the tradition of invention—of inventing the king as Rāma—begins in the twelfth century' (263). The two centuries, starting with the twelfth century, are, in Pollock's opinion, crucial for the invention of the king as Rāma and for the growing centrality of the cult of Rāma as enshrined in temples. The historical context for both is provided by the beginning and crystallization of Turkish rule in India; the representation of the king as Rāma and Rāma devotion in religious sphere are projected as a kind of national response (since it is viewed as 'public') to 'foreign' rule of the Turuṣkas. Since the response is formed by adopting the idiom of the *Rāmāyaṇa,* the image of the Turuṣka embedded in the public, political imagination is that of the demon (*rākṣasa*). The suggested historical causation is not original; it will be seen presently that in tracing the history of Rāma devotion in north India Hans Bakker too made this causal connection, although somewhat casually in the beginning but more firmly later. Pollock's argument, however, goes much beyond making the causal connection; in his construction, Rāma becomes central to a situation of an 'utter dichotomization of the enemy' (283) in the society of early medieval and medieval India.

In substantiating and explaining the invention of the king as Rāma and the growth of Rāma devotion, Pollock has used evidence from architecture, epigraphy (of the variety labelled as 'political inscriptions') and texts. What we propose to do now is to take each category of Pollock's evidence and examine its weightage in the light of comparable evidence available for the period. Pollock contends: 'The Rāma cult in South Asia is almost totally nonexistent until at the earliest the eleventh, or more likely the twelfth century, and the growth of this cult took place in virtual synchrony with a set of particular historical events' (265). It has already been mentioned that Pollock is not alone in making the causal connection between 'a set of particular historical events' and the growth of the cult of Rāma. Hans Bakker too had postulated the emergence of the worship of Rāma 'in the latest period of independent Hindu rule in north India' and before the firm establishment of Muslim power.[3] Bakker believed that while other *avātara* cults of Viṣṇu were based on regional, popular and not specifically Vaiṣṇava traditions, the expansion of Rāma cult had to wait for *'favourable* historical circumstances' [emphasis mine]: 'This seems to have occurred when Hindus were driven into a defensive position by Muslim power, but this factor would never have led to a cult of such dimensions, impact and

[3] Hans Bakker, *Ayodhyā,* pt. I, Groningen, 1986, p. 66.

importance, had not a wave of emotional devotion (*bhakti*) of a particular kind completely transformed the outlook and character of Hindu religion, in particular of Vaiṣṇavism.'[4] Although Bakker continued to talk about the 'evolution of emotional devotion of Kṛṣṇa and Rāma into a mass movement' by the Mughal period and about the impact of Sufism and Nātha Yogism on it, historiographically, methodologically, and taken in conjunction with Pollock's position, this statement of Bakker is significantly different from his earlier statement in that it has moved away from his earlier emphasis on emotional bhakti:

When we try to relate the foregoing evidence to the contemporary Sanskrit literature, *we note that the paucity of Rāmaite texts matches the scarcity of Rāma temples*. Yet, there are a few texts which endorse the view that the development of Rāma devotion, rather than originating as a popular cult that became accepted by the higher classes of society, was a current within 'higher' Hinduism in which Rāma was substituted for Viṣṇu and conceived of as his supreme embodiment. This movement gained momentum among the members of the ruling class who were evidently supported by a section of the Brahmanical fold. In this connection we should note that the figure of Rāma, the ideal of righteousness (*dharma*), majestic splendour and valour (*kṣatra*), lent itself perfectly to the role of principal diety, a symbol of the desperate Hindu struggle against a new and uncompromising power that threatened to subvert its traditional pattern and values. . . . It might therefore be more than just coincidence that the archaeological remains of Rāma sanctuaries and epigraphical evidence testifying to Rāma devotion are found in septentrional India, in particular in the mountainous districts of Madhya Pradesh and Maharashtra that temporarily functioned as a buffer zone between the Muslim advance and traditional Hindu society. The physical character of the terrain, difficult of access and a hindrance to effective control, spared some of the Hindu edifices from total oblivion.[5] [emphasis mine]

In this ecology of Rāma sanctuaries and the newly accentuated causation, emotional devotion is not even given the benefit of a doubt.

The evidence presented by Pollock, which is taken to contrast with representations of *Rāmāyaṇa* themes in pre-twelfth century temples, consists of inscriptional references of the twelfth century to two temples dedicated to Rāma in the kingdom of the Kalacuris of Ratanpur in the Chhattisgarh area of Madhya Pradesh, the Rāma complex at Ramtek and the Rāmacandra shrine at Hampi in the kingdom of Vijayanagara (266–9). Although Pollock talks about 'several major cultic centres devoted to Rāma' being 'created or reinvigorated' at the end of the thirteenth and the beginning of the fourteenth

[4] Ibid.

[5] Hans Bakker, 'Reflections on the Evolution of Rāma Devotion in the Light of Textual and Archaeological Evidence', *Wiener Zeitschrift fur die Kunde Südasiens und Archiv für Indische Philosophie*, Band XXXI, 1987, pp. 20–1.

centuries, he does not specify what they were. He is not sure himself what the situation in the Gāhaḍavāla kingdom of Uttar Pradesh was like; he refers to Bakker's work on Ayodhya to point out that the 'Gāhaḍavāla dynasty begins to develop Ayodhya as a major Vaiṣṇava center by way of a substantial temple building program' (266). Although no definite inscriptional evidence is forthcoming, Pollock would nevertheless like to believe that 'a Rāma temple was constructed at Svargadvara ghat, probably by Jayacandra. (And was a birth place temple built by the last Gāhaḍavāla king, Jayacandra?).'[6]

By standards of 'objectivist' history which Pollock derides but to the method of which he has resorted, rather weakly, the evidence, considering the significant growth of temple building activities all over India from the Gupta period onward, is decidedly thin. Whether one takes inscriptional references to the sectarian character of the temples built or the evidence of the temples themselves, it would certainly not require an expert on religious history or on temple architecture to tell us that in the adequate documentation available so far, it is temples of Śiva and Viṣṇu, and comparatively less significantly, those of other deities which would constitute the majority.[7] If numbers do not matter, one wonders in what terms exactly one can establish the growing centrality of the cult of Rāma. Pollock's supposition that 'the apogee of the growth of a royal cult of Rāma . . . is reached in the middle [or end] of the fourteenth century with the founding of the Vijayanagar empire in the Deccan' (267) is again premised on the weight of his elusive 'royal cult of Rāma' in pre-fourteenth century period. Although the Rāmacandra temple was located in the nucleus of the royal complex at Vijayanagara, Pollock too finds it difficult to consider it as the shrine of the *rāṣṭradevatā* of Vijayanagara,

[6] The correct spelling of the name is Jayaccandra. Gāhaḍavāla rule did not end immediately after Jayaccandra. It may be noted that according to Jaina *Prabandhakośa*, Jayantacandra (Gāhaḍavāla Jayaccandra) lost his kingdom to the Muslim overlord of Takṣaśilā who was invited, by Jayantacandra's concubine, with offer of a huge amount of gold, to come and destroy Vārāṇasī. See Phyllis Granoff, ed., *The Clever Adulteress and Other Stories: A Treasury of Jain Literature*, Oakville, New York and London, 1990, pp. 161–2.

[7] For forming an impression about the sectarian affiliations of numerous temples constructed in the early medieval period, it is necessary to wade through a vast mass of epigraphic and architectural evidence. R.K. Chattopadhyaya was kind enough to go through, with me, a number of relevant recent publications on early medieval temples and confirm my initial impressions. For a preliminary idea, the following recent publications may be cited: Krishna Deva, *Temples of India*, vol. I (Text), Delhi, 1996, *passim*, and Site and Temple Index; M.W. Meister, ed., *Encyclopaedia of Indian Temple Architecture; South India: Lower Dravidadesa*, Delhi, 1983; see also the architectural survey by S.K. Saraswati in R.C. Majumdar, ed.. *The Struggle for Empire (The History and Culture of the Indian People)*, Bombay, 1957, Chap. 20.

the cult centre repeatedly mentioned in the official epigraphic records of the Vijayanagara kings being that of Virūpākṣa.[8] In fact, the following is the kind of sacred landscape which a Vijayanagara inscription would present:

He performed various gifts at the Golden Hall (Chidāmbaram), at the shrine of holy Virūpākṣadeva, at the town of the holy lord of Kalahasti, on Veṅkaṭādri, at Kānchī, at Śrīśaila, at Śoṇaśaila, at the sacred (city of) Harihara, at Ahobala, at Saṅgama, at Śrīranga, at Kumbhaghoṇa, at the sinless *tīrtha* of Mahānandi (and) Nivṛtti.[9]

Compare this with the landscape of sacred centres in late thirteenth–early fourteenth centuries Andhra:

The land extending from the Southern Ocean to the king of mountains (*Himālayas*) was known as Bhāratavarsha . . . in that was situated the land of the Andhras, otherwise called Triliṅga-bhūmi by its association with three famous shrines (*lingas*), viz. Śrīśaila, Kāleśvara and Dākṣārāma. . . . Therein are the five gardens (*aratnas*) namely Dāksha, Amara, Kshīra, Kumāra and Prāchya, the sporting grounds of Śiva and the holy rivers such as Gautamī (*Godāvarī*), Krishṇaveṇī, Malapahā, Bhīmarathī and Tuṅgabhadrā. . . . On the bank of the river Krishṇā is Śrīkakula, the abode of Vishnu (Śrīvallabha) for the protection of the three worlds.[10]

Both the Vijayanagara and Andhra inscriptions were written in the heyday of Turuṣka penetration into the Deccan. In fact, there is a number of fourteenth-century inscriptions from Andhra, which portray in vivid colours the predicament of the Andhra people because of Turuṣka invasions and

[8] Anila Verghese too underlines the importance of the Rāmacandra temple as a royal temple, but distinguishes it from the guardian deity of the State: 'Pampa Virūpāksha has undoubtedly been the principal deity at the site from before the founding of the empire onwards, and he was adopted as the guardian deity of the Vijayanagara State.' Anila Verghese, *Religious Traditions in Vjayanagara: As Revealed Through its Monuments*, Delhi, 1995, p. 132. Verghese finds no evidence of a Rāma temple at Vijayanagara before the early fifteenth century and associates the growth of Vaiṣṇava cults—those of Rāma and Viṭhala—with vigorous Mādhva and Śrīvaṣṇava activity during the late fifteenth and sixteenth centuries; ibid. The statement of Pollock, therefore, is again misleading: 'Governors of the Delhi Sultanate were appointed throughout the Deccan, and soon thereafter the Vijayanagara Kingdom was established (1346), with a Rāma temple at its city core' (279). G. Michell, on the other hand, believes that the nucleus of Vijayanagara's early sacred centre at Hampi consisted of Saivite shrines; examples of early Vijayanagara shrines in the Telugu zone were: Mādhavarāya Temple at Gorantla near Penukonda and Mallikārjuna at Śrīsailam; see G. Michell, *Architecture and Art of Southern India*, The New Cambridge History of India 1:6, Cambridge, 1995, pp. 31–2.

[9] E. Hultzsch, 'Hampi Inscription of Krishnaraya, Dated Śaka 1430', *EI*, vol. 1, pp. 361–71.

[10] K.H.V. Sarma and T. Krishnamurty, 'Annavarappadu Plates of Kataya Vema Reddy', *EI*, vol. 36, p. 168.

rule, and also the achievements of the local heroes in liberating them.[11] The 'political imagination' which these inscriptions display has no reference to Rāma; their sacred landscape is projected in terms of what had emerged by then as the major sacred sites of the region.

When one considers the royal cults of the early medieval period, in so far as a list of such centres can be prepared on the basis of epigraphy and actual sites, what should strike one as significant is their distinct variety. If Bṛhadīśvara and Gaṅgaikoṇḍacolapuram could be regarded as royal cult centres respectively of Rājarāja and Rājendra among the Colas of Tamilnadu,[12] then the epigraphs and also the coins of the Kadambas of Goa consistently refer to Śrīsaptakoṭīśvara as their deity;[13] the Śilāhāras of Kolhapur invoked Mahalaksmi in their inscriptions,[14] the Caulukyas and Vāghelas of Gujarat appear to have considered Somanatha as their most important deity.[15] In Rajasthan, the site of Ekaliṅga was gradually emerging as a major centre of royal cult in the kingdom of the Guhilas of Mewar;[16] in Orissa, the Bhanjas worshipped Śiva and Stambheśvarī,[17] and, as is well known, the cult of Jagannātha with which the entire region came to be later identified exemplified the royal cult par excellence from the time of the Coḍagaṅgas onward.[18] These are only a few examples, but even so, viewed from this new historical process of the formation of royal and regional cults, which cannot be pinned down to any particular century, the evidence adduced by Bakker and Pollock does not appear extraordinarily significant and may have to be explained in ways other than what have been advocated by them.

I would like to make two further points before moving on to the next section; one relating to the iconography of the king who is supposed to have been 'invented as Rāma', and the second relating to the iconography

[11] See Chap. 2 of this volume.

[12] For the Colas see K.A. Nilakanta Sastri, *The Colas*, 2nd edn., Madras, repr. 1975, Chaps. 9–10.

[13] G.M. Moraes, *The Kadamba Kula: A History of Ancient and Medieval Karnataka*, Bombay, 1931.

[14] V.V. Mirashi, *Inscriptions of the Śilāhāras*, Corpus Inscriptionum Indicarum, Delhi, 1977, p. XLIX.

[15] See, for example, G. Bühler, 'Eleven Landgrants of the Chaulukyas of Anhilvadi: A Contribution to the History of Gujarat', *IA*, vol. 6, 1877, pp. 180–214.

[16] Nandini Sinha, 'A Study of State and Cult: The Guhilas, Pasupatas and Ekalingaji in Mewar, Seventh to Fifteenth Centuries AD', *Studies in History*, vol. 9, no. 2, 1993, pp. 161–82.

[17] The usual expression in inscriptions is: *Slambheśvarī-labdha-varaprasāda*, see S. Tripathi, *Inscriptions of Orissa*, vol. 6, Bhuvaneswar, 1974, pp. 67, 73, 79.

[18] A. Eschmann, H. Kulke, G.C. Tripathi, eds., *The Cult of Jagannath and The Regional Tradition of Orissa*, Delhi, 1978, *passim*.

of Rāma. Whatever little is available of the iconography of the king in early medieval and medieval art does not indicate the invention of the king as archer Rāma—a development which was expected in terms of Pollock's argument.[19] Pollock's use of two illustrations, one of a contemporary rightwing politician as Rāma and the other of Pṛthvīrāja III Cāhamāna[20] is again misleading because of his suggested hint of continuity from the early medieval period. The first is indeed the invention of journalism; the second, of Cāhamāna Pṛthvīrāja III, as an archer, belongs to the early nineteenth century and may have nothing to do with Rāma. If the representation of a king as an archer was intended to convey his invariable identity as Rāma, then the Gupta kings figuring as archers on their coins should all surely have to be considered as Rāma.[21] Second, regarding the iconography of Rāma in the context of the representation of *Rāmāyaṇa* themes in art, one may cite, as a sample, P. Banerjee's work titled *Rāma in Indian Literature, Art and Thought.*[22]

[19] Royal portrait sculptures are not available in plenty, but even so reference may be made to a few: (1) Rajendra, the Cola ruler, receiving a floral garland of victory from Śiva at Gangaikondacolapuram (G. Michell, *The Hindu Temple: An Introduction to its Meaning and Form*, Chicago, 1988, p. 17); (2) the Coḍagaṅga ruler at Konarak. Of several representations of Narasiṃha, the Orissan ruler of the thirteenth century at Konark, only one is that of an archer (collections at the National Museum, New Delhi and the photo-archives of the Archaeological Survey of India): (3) Candella ruler and his consort as worshippers: Devangana Desai, *The Religious Imagery of Khajuraho*, Mumbai, 1996, p. xxviii; (4) Kṛṣṇadevarāya: represented as a worshipper at north Gopura at Chidambaram (George Michell, *Architecture and Art of Southern India: Vijayanagara and the Successor States*, The New Cambridge History of India, 1.6, Cambridge, 1995, pp. 158–9, fig. 114].

The observations of Anila Verghese on the iconography of the king and of Rāma at Vijayanagara would be pertinent in this context: 'If the king in Vijayanagara is identified with Rāma, in turn Rāma is also portrayed as a king. This is to be found in certain reliefs in the temples, which is at variance with the traditionally accepted iconographic representations of this god. In these unusual reliefs, Rāma is shown sitting on a throne-like seat, leaning against a cushion or bolster, with one leg crossed over the other, often with one hand raised in the *tarjanī-mudrā* (one finger pointing upwards) and usually with a shawl draped around one arm. He is depicted exactly as the kings are on the enclosure walls of the Rāmachandra temple complex, on the Mahanavami platform and elsewhere. The only difference is in the headdress: while the god wears the *Kirīṭamukuṭa,* the typical crown worn by Viṣṇu in his diverse manifestations, the kings are bareheaded or wear the *Kullāyi':* Verghese, op. cit., p. 51, pls. 19, 20. In iconography, neither the god, nor the king is Kodaṇḍa-Rāma.

[20] Pollock, pp. 290–1.

[21] For Gupta kings as archers see John Allan, *Catalogue of the Coins of the Gupta Dynasties and of Śaśāṅka, King of Gauḍa*, London, repr. 1967, pp. 6–7, 24–33, 61–6, etc.

[22] P. Banerji, *Rāma in Indian Literature, Art and Thought,* 2 vols. (text and illustrations), Delhi, 1986.

The total number of illustrations included in the work is 286; dated between the early historical period and the nineteenth century, the illustrations do not indicate any preference for a particular kind of icon at any historical stage; on the other hand, they relate to a wide variety of themes in the *Rāmāyaṇa* story. Of the 286 illustrations, seven depict the fight between Rāma and Rāvaṇa;[23] of these six belong to the period between the sixteenth and the nineteenth centuries, although, since they occur alongside representations of different other *Rāmāyaṇa* themes, one cannot see how any particular significance can be attached to this.

III

Pollock's second category of evidence consists of inscriptions which, it may be mentioned in the beginning, increase manifold in number from the Gupta period onward and of which thousands are available. Pollock relates the 'public discourse of major dynasties', as articulated in their inscriptions, to the 'appropriation of the Rāma theme' (271) from the twelfth century. He refers to a few inscriptions datable upto the twelfth century and feels that till that stage 'Rāma and *Rāmāyaṇa* mythemes function as peripheral rhetorical embellishments, inflecting and texturing a given discourse but not constituting it' (272). By contrast, 'the later-period political world comes to be read through—identified with, cognized by—the narrative provided by the epic tale' (272). Two inscriptions are cited to support this supposition about the envisioned political world: (1) the Dabhoi stone inscription (AD 1253) of the Vāghela family of Gujarat, and (2) Hansi inscription of 1167, which may be regarded as a *praśasti* of Cāhamāna Pṛthvīrāja II.

The Dabhoi inscription[24] refers to *Gurjara rājya,* ruled over by Lavaṇaprasāda, as greater than *Ramarājya* and to the defeat of the Turuṣka king, dreaded by other kings, by Lavaṇaprasāda, who, the inscription asserts, could not be a mere mortal. However, the 'meaning-conjuncture'—an expression which Pollock has used to point to the identity of the king as victor over the Turuṣkas with Rāma, the slayer of Rāvaṇa—does not take place in this record. Lavaṇaprasāda surely defeated the Turuṣka king, but as his *Gurjara rājya* was perceived as greater than the model *Ramarājya.* he was not being identified as Rāma. Indeed, other details of the record, not mentioned by Pollock, are worth taking note of in this context. The inscription was composed to record the construction, by the reigning king Vīsaladeva, of a temple of Kumāra at Vardhamāna, of several temples of

[23] Ibid., pp. 202, 204–9.

[24] G. Bühler, 'An Inscription from Dabhoi', *EI*, vol. I, pp. 20–32.

Śiva, of the restoration of a Sun temple called Mūlasthāna and of another temple which 'resembled a peak of the mountain of Hara'. The record refers to Arṇoraja, founder of the Vāghela line, as imitating the feats of Kṛṣṇa; however, his adversary Raṇasiṃha, slain on battlefield, was like Rāvaṇa. Lavaṇaprasāda, victor over the Turuṣka king, is mentioned as of greater fame than Yudhiṣṭhira, and his son Vīradhavala was 'the image of Daśaratha and Kākustha'. The composer of the record obviously drew upon a repertoire of available motifs from both epics, and the inscription offers no evidence of Pollock's desired 'meaning-conjuncture'.

The Hansi record of 1167 from Haryana does institute an identification, through the mediacy of an enigmatic Vibhisana, of Cāhamāna king Pṛthvīrāja with Rāma and of Kilhaṇa,[25] Pṛthvīrāja's maternal uncle, with Hanuman.[26] One will, however, need to locate the evidence of the Hansi record in the comparable contexts of many other contemporary inscriptions.

It has been mentioned in our text that in the repertoire of divine and legendary figures with whom our heroes are identified, the liberator is usually Viṣṇu or Mahāvarāha who lifts the earth submerged in the ocean of Turuṣka rule; one also comes across Agastya as the swallower of the ocean.[27] However, in the early medieval epigraphs, whether in the context of Yavana raids or outside them, the king as a hero and a ruler has many identities: Indra, Viṣṇu, Viṣṇu Trivikrama, Mahāvarāha, Śiva, Pṛthu, Agastya, Kāma, Revanta, Yudhiṣṭhira, Bhīma, Rāma and so on. The use of the legendary figure of Rāma and the reference to his ideal rule are a part of a complex of motifs, and there is never any suggestion in the records themselves that a particular motif gains precedence over others in a specific context. Let me illustrate this point by juxtaposing extracts from a few early medieval inscriptions:

1. Miraj Plates of Śilāhāra Mārasiṃha, AD 1058: 'The king Mārasiṃha resembles Revanta (and) Udayana in respect of excellent horse-riding, and Bhīma by his terrible valour; . . . he is the god of love in respect of beautiful form, . . . and by his deeds he resembles Rāma and other primeval (great) kings.'[28]

[25] Pollock wrongly identifies (and therefore wrongly discovers mistake in the spelling of the name Kelhaṇa) Kilhaṇa who was a Guhilāuta (Guhila) and maternal uncle of Cāhamāna Pṛthvīrāja with Naddula Cāhamāna Kelhaṇa.

[26] D.R. Bhandarkar, 'Hansi Stone Inscription of Prithviraja, Vikrama Samvat 1224', *IA*, vol. 41, 1912, pp. 17–19.

[27] N. Venkataramanayya and M. Somasekhara Sharma, 'Vilasa Grant of Prolaya Nayaka', *EI*, vol. 32, 1957–8, Delhi, repr. 1987, p. 253, fn. 3.

[28] Mirashi, *Inscriptions of the Śilāhāras*, pp. 200ff.

2. Machchishahr Copperplate inscription, AD 1197: 'To whom was born a king called Vijayacandra (son of Gāhaḍavāla Govindacandra) who was capable of destroying the allies of enemy kings; just as Indra is capable of cutting as under the wings of the (fabulous flying) mountains and who (Indra), had washed off the heat of the terrestrial world with streams of water from the clouds in the shape of the eyes of the Hammīra women, when he was indulging in the sport of subduing the world (?).'[29]
3. Chaudharapada Stone inscription of Keśideva II, Śilāhāra king of north Konkan, AD 1240: 'Having seen the mode of administration of him who is a store of immeasurable and holy valour, the divine earth does not remember (with regret) (the ancient) kings such as Rāma.'[30]
4. Ajaygadh rock inscription of Candella Viravarman, AD 1261: '. . . Pṛthvīvarman was king, similar to Pṛthu; and then Madana ruled over the kingdom, a god of love to the opponents. Then came the illustrious king Paramārdin, who, as a leader, even in his youth, struck down opposing heroes. . . . Then the prince Trailokyavarman ruled the kingdom, a very creator in providing strong places. Like Viṣṇu he was, in lifting up the earth, immerged in the ocean formed by the streams of Turuṣkas. Victorious is his son Vira, that ruler of the earth of spotless bravery who has delighted the damsels of heaven by sending them, as lovers, the hostile heroes whom he cut down on the field of battle. Victorious (and) to be worshipped by all men is he whom, when he strikes down the wicked (and) disperses crowds of opponents, people gaze at—wondering whether he be Viṣṇu riding on Garuḍa or Śiva about on his Bull.'[31]

These few samples should suffice to show that Pollock has arbitrarily isolated Rāma in relation to a specific context from the variegated world of the model divinities and legendary kings as he has isolated one *rākṣasa/asura* by avoiding reference to others.

IV

Pollock's last category of evidence is what he calls 'historiographical' or 'textualized' (273). The evidence is provided by two texts: *Prabandha Cintāmaṇi* of Merutuṅga and *Pṛthvīrāja-vijaya* of Jayānaka (*c.*1190–2). Both texts consider their respective kings, Jayasiṃha Siddharāja and Pṛthvīrāja III

[29] P. Prasad, *Sanskrit Inscrptions of Delhi Sultanate 1191–1526*, Delhi, 1990, pp. 58-70.

[30] Mirashi, *Inscriptions of the Śilāhāras*, pp. 169–72.

[31] F. Kielhorn, 'Two Chandella Stone Inscriptions from Ajaygadh', *EI*, vol. I, pp. 325–30.

Cāhamāna as incarnations of Rāma, and the text *Pṛthvīrāja-vijaya* in particular dwells at length on the depredations by the Turuṣkas in the region of Ajayameru in Rajasthan. This apparently lends incontestable support to Pollock's supposition of 'mythopolitical equivalence' (275).

I have cited enough evidence from inscriptions by now to show that in the early medieval period there were different ways of making comparisons and that, therefore, there was more than one pattern to the invocation of equivalence. For example, Turuṣka depredations and textual representation of cultural difference, it must be noted, are not unique to *Pṛthvīrāja-vijaya;* the *Madhurā-vijaya* and the Vilasa Grant, cited in the text,[32] have comparable details but do not seem to lend support to Pollock's particular brand of 'mythopolitical equivalence'. This of course is another illustration of Pollock's method, i.e. to generalize on the basis of select evidence without bothering to find out whether evidence exists to contradict it. Marginalization of Sandhyākara Nandi's *Rāma-carita*—which too does not suit his hypothesis—is another example.[33]

A synchronic view of texts, advocated by us, would involve looking for different patterns in disparate material which nevertheless was the product of the same age. A synchronic view of texts—epigraphical and literary—of the early medieval period concerning kings would suggest that the discourse on monarchy was constituted by attempts to construct images of the king: (1) as hero and conqueror in which the motif of *digvijaya* is significantly present; (2) as an ideal ruler; (3) as protector. The meanings of individual texts and of the wide range of images in them can appear compatible only with reference to this general discourse. References to concrete historical events elaborated the major points in this discourse; attempts to arrive at a particular 'mytho-political equivalence' through a minimal correlation of the reasonably secure (and generally well-known) historical record of the invasions' (277) with select evidence can be made, as it has been made by Pollock, by completely ignoring the broad textual meanings of different dimensions of king and monarchy.

[32] See Chap. 2 of this volume.

[33] Cf. Pollock (283): 'True the Cālukyas could imagine the Colas as *rākṣasas,* or the Colas could thus position the Sinhalese. Conversely, other evidence does show that non-*Rāmāyaṇa* mythemes could on occasion be used to narrate the encounter with the Central Asians.' It is, however, not enough to refer to the other evidence; one expects to learn how the evidence cited is intellgible in the light of the hypothesis offered or whether it is simply negligible aberration. Similarly, Pollock does not offer to explain how his evidence (285) which may demonstrate a 'sustained and largely successful effort at intercultural translation' can be reconciled with his notion of 'the utter dichotomization of the enemy' (283).

It is reference to this general discourse which may be helpful in understanding the growing incorporation of Rāma and his rule in texts which arc concerned with monarchy. Instead of focusing on Pollock's rather limited 'imaginary resources' (281) of the *Rāmāyaṇa* as provider of images of 'Divine' and 'Demon', let us examine the relevance of Rāma for a general monarchical discourse:

Since ancient times the term *Rāma-rājya* 'The kingship of Rāma' represents the Indian concept of an ideal state. It originates in Vālmīki's *Rāmāyaṇa,* the well known Sanskrit epic of King Rāma of Ayodhyā. In the course of time the Sanskrit *Rāmāyaṇa* was translated and reworked in a number of other—both south and north Indian—languages. These translations and adaptations of the Sanskrit *Rāmāyaṇa* especially took place in connection with the movement of Bhakti which focussed on a personal love of God. Within this context the character of Rāma, the hero of the Sanskrit *Rāmāyaṇa,* underwent a significant change. He was no longer regarded as a human king but came to the viewed as an *avatāra* 'incarnation' of the god Viṣṇu. As a result, Rāma assumed the character of a king/god.[34]

While this rather 'conventional' view effectively suggests that there are historical movements, apart from political events alone, which too can offer insights for 'minimal correlation', the suitability of the *Rāmāyaṇa* in the discourse of monarchy and its textual representation comes out further in Smith's book:

Both the *Mahābhārata* and the *Rāmāyaṇa* are concerned with abiding problems for kings: palace intrigue, determining the heir to the throne, and being a good ruler. The *Mahābhārata,* despite all its mythology, is a profoundly realistic work for the modern reader, for its pessimism, in the failure of the righteous Yudhiṣṭhira to reign satisfactorily. Although the *Rāmāyaṇa,* the first *Kavya,* is considered the elder epic by Indian tradition, it is in fact well on the way to being a court epic, and this not only on account of its more polished style. *Ramarājya,* Rāma's royal rule, is the perfect political state, in the view of all succeeding ages because Valmiki, the first poet, set out to make it so. . . . This shaping, this loss of heroic ruggedness, no doubt explains why subsequent poets often retell the whole *Rāmāyaṇa* but select only single episodes of the *Mahābhārata.*[35]

It was in the logic of historical change in India then that the discourse of monarchy was to hinge largely on the *Rāmāyaṇa* this was its essential 'imaginative resource'. I have elsewhere tried to argue that the final

[34] A.G. Menon and G.H. Schokker, 'The Concept of Rāmārājya in South and North Indian Literature', in *Ritual, State and History in South Asia: Essays in Honour of J.C. Heesterman,* ed. A.W. van Den Hoek. D.H.A. Kolff and M.S. Oort, p. 615.

[35] David Smith, *Ratnākara's Haravijaya: An Introduction to the Sanskrit Court Epic,* Delhi, 1985, pp. 14–15.

resolution of the tension between non-monarchical and monarchical systems of governance was resolved during the Gupta period; the pace of the proliferation of local kingly power through the process of local-level state formation; crystallization of regional kingdoms and the triumph of monarchical ideology were all developments of the post-Gupta period which substantially changed the political landscape of India and underlined the centrality of *Varṇāśramadharma* in the monarchical discourse.[36] This spatial expansion of what we have called state society, during centuries following the Gupta period, was the historical context in which the growing importance of Rāma and the *Rāmāyaṇa* has to be located; in this state society, defined by *Varṇāśramadharma,* the Yavanas or the Mlecchas, as social groups, would always be outsiders and would be perceived as others. To link Rāma and the *Rāmāyaṇa* not to this vision of the ideal state but to invasions alone would be at the cost of sidelining the broad processes of historical change which integrated disparate regions of India through the centuries marked by the emergence of large regional states of early medieval times.

One final point. There cannot, perhaps, be any disagreement with Pollock that analysis of ways in which meanings are created and promulgated in history is a more worthwhile historical enterprise than attempts at simply unravelling the authenticity, or otherwise, of historical events. But perhaps the historical, objective 'reality' of meanings is as elusive—and dubious—as the reality of historical events themselves. The quality of investigation into meanings will also be contingent upon the contemporary privileged position of the investigator with the particular ideological position he may choose to take or espouse; Pollock has demonstrated how contemporary communal consciousness can be traced back directly to the early medieval phase of Indian history and that a construction of the history of communal consciousness does not have to make any reference to its colonial phase. The past, one cannot help feeling after confronting this 'originary', will ever remain a dumb victim of its wily investigators.

[36] B.D. Chattopadhyaya, *The Making of Early Medieval India,* Delhi, 1994, Chaps. 1 and 8. Also idem, 'Historiography, History and Religious Centers: Early Medieval North India, Circa AD 700-1200', in *Gods, Guardians and Lovers: Temple Sculptures from North India AD 700-1200,* ed. Vishakha N. Desai and Darielle Mason, New York and Ahmedabad, 1993, pp. 33–47.

Select Bibliography

Aiyangar, K.V. Rangaswami, ed., *Kṛtyakalpataru of Bhaṭṭa Lakṣmīdhara,* vol. 5 (*Dānakāṇḍa*), Baroda, 1941.

Bakker, Hans, *Ayodhyā,* pt. I, Groningen, 1986.

______, 'Reflections on the Evolution of Rāma Devotion in the Light of Textual and Archaeological Evidence', *Wiener Zeitschrift für die Kunde Südasiens und Archiv für Indische Philosophie,* Band XXXI, 1987, pp. 9–42.

Banerji, P., *Rāma in Indian Literature, Art and Thought,* 2 vols. (text and illustrations), Delhi, 1986.

Bayly, Susan, *Saints, Goddesses and Kings: Muslims and Christians in South Indian Society 1700–1900,* Indian edn., Delhi, 1992.

Bhandarkar, D.R.,'Hansi Stone Inscription of Prithvirāja, Vikrama Samvat 1224', *IA,* vol. 41, 1912, pp. 17–19.

______, 'Pārasīka Dominion in Ancient India', *Annals of the Bhandarkar Oriental Research Institute,* vol. 8, 1926–7, pp. 133–41.

______, 'A List of Inscriptions', *Appendix to Epigraphia Indica and Record of the Archaeological Survey of India,* vols. 19-23, Delhi; repr. 1983.

Bühler, G. 'An Inscription from Dabhoi', *EI,* vol. I, Delhi, repr. 1983, pp. 20–32.

______, 'The Kangra Jwalamukhi Prasasti, *EI,* vol. I, Delhi, 1983, pp. 190–5.

______, *'The Jagaḍūcharita of Sarvāṇanda: A Historical Romance from Gujarat,* Indian Studies, no. 1, Wien, 1892.

______, 'Eleven Landgrants of the Chaulukyas of Anahilabad: A Contribution to the History of Gujarat', *IA,* vol. 6, 1877, pp. 180–214.

Bukhari, Y.K., 'Inscriptions from the Archaeological Museum, Red Fort, Delhi', *EI:* Arabic and Persian Supplement 1959-61, Delhi, 1987, no. 6, pp. 8–10.

Chandra Prabha, *Historical Mahākāvyas in Sanskrit (Eleventh to Fifteenth Century AD)*, Delhi, 1976.

Chatterjee, Partha, 'Claims on the Past: The Genealogy of Modern Historiography in Bengal", in *Subaltern Studies VIII: Essays in Honour of Ranajit Guha*, ed. David Arnold and David Hardiman, 2nd ptg., Delhi, 1995, pp. 1–49.

Chattopadhyaya, B.D., 'Historigraphy, History and Religious Centers: Early Medieval North India, Circa AD 700-1200', in *Gods, Guardians and Lovers: Temple Sculpture from North India, AD 700-1200*, ed. Vishakha N. Desai and Darielle Mason, New York and Ahmedabad, 1993, pp. 33–47.

———, *The Making of Early Medieval India*, Delhi, 1994, Chaps. 1 and 8.

Desai, M.D., *Bhānucandra Caritra by his Pupil Gaṇi Siddhicandra Upādhyāya*, Ahmedabad and Calcutta, 1941.

Desai, Z.A., 'Muslims in the 13th Century Gujarat, as Known from Arabic Inscriptions', *Journal of Oriental Institute*, vol. 10, Baroda, 1960–1, pp. 353–64.

Eaton, R., *The Rise of Islam and the Bengal Frontier, 1204–1760*, Delhi, 1994.

Eggeling, J., 'Sarban Inscription in the Delhi Museum', *EI*, vol. 1, 1892, Delhi, 1983, pp. 93–5.

Elliot, H.M. and J. Dowson, *The History of India as Told by its Own Historians* (*The Muhammadan Period*), vol. 2, Allahabad, repr. n.d.

Ghosh, A. and R.S. Avasthy, 'References to Muhammadans in Sanskrit Inscriptions in Northern India, AD 730 to 1320', *Journal of Indian History*, vol. 15, 1936, pp. 161–84; vol. 16, 1937–8, pp. 24–6.

Gokhale, Sobhana, *Kanheri Inscriptions*, Poona, 1991.

Golzio, Karl-Heinz, 'Das Problem von Toleranz and Intoleranz in Indischen Religionen anhand Epigraphischer Quellen', in *Frank-Richard Hamm Memorial Volume*, ed. Helmut Eimer, Bonn, 1990, pp. 89–102.

Granoff, Phyllis, ed., *The Clever Adulteress and Other Stories: A Treasury of Jain Literature*, Oakville, New York and London, 1990.

Hira Lal, 'Batihagarh Stone Inscription, Samvat 1385', *EI*, vol. 12, 1913–14, Delhi, repr. 1982, pp. 44–7.

———, 'Burhanpur Sanskrit Inscription of Adil Shah, Samvat 1646', *EI*, vol. 9, 1907–8, Delhi, repr. 1981, pp. 306–10.

Hultzsch, E., 'A Grant of Arjunadeva of Gujarat, Dated 1264 AD', *IA*, vol. 11, 1882, pp. 241–5.

———, 'Four Inscriptions of Kulottuṅga Chola', *EI*, vol. 5, Delhi, repr. 1984, p. 104.

———, 'Hampe Inscription of Krishnaraya, Dated Śaka 1430', *EI*, vol. I, pp. 361–71.

Hussain, Anwar, 'The "Foreigner" and the Indian Society (circa Eighth Century to Thirteenth Century): A Study of Epigraphic Evidence from Northern and Western India', M.Phil. dissertation, Centre for Historical Studies, Jawaharlal Nehru University, 1993.

Hussain, M.D., *A Study of Nineteenth Century Historical Works on Muslim Rule in Bengal: Charles Stuart to Henry Beveridge*, Dhaka, 1987.

Jain, U., 'Umariya Plates of Vijayasiṃhadeva', *EI*, vol. 41, 1975–6, Delhi, 1989, pp. 38–48.

Joshi, M.C., 'Some Nagari Inscriptions on the Qutb Minar', *Medieval India: A Miscellany*, vol. 2, Aligarh, 1972, pp. 3–6.

Joshi, Sashi and B.S. Josh, *Struggle for Hegemony in India 1920-47: Culture, Community and Power*, vol. 3, 1941–7, Delhi, 1994.

Kane, P.V., 'The Pahlavas and Pārasīkas in Ancient Sanskrit Literature', in *Dr Modi Memorial Volume*, ed. Dr Modi Memorial Volume Editorial Board, Bombay, 1930, pp. 352–7.

———, *History of Dharmaśāstra (Ancient and Medieval Religious and Civil Law in India*, vol. 4, Poona, 1953.

Kaul Deambi, B.K., *Corpus of Śāradā Inscriptions of Kashmir*, Delhi, 1982, pp. 113–18.

Kielhorn, F., 'Khalimpur Plate of Dharmapaladeva', *EI*, vol. 4, Delhi, repr. 1979, pp. 243–54.

———, 'Two Chandella Stone Inscriptions from Ajaygarh', *EI*, vol. I, pp. 325–30.

Krishnamacharya, Embar, ed., *Rāshṭrauḍhavaṇśa Kāvya of Rudrakavi*, with an Introduction by C.D. Dalai, Gaekwad's Oriental Series, no. 5, Baroda, 1917.

Majumdar, R.C., ed., *The Classical Age*, vol. 3 of *The History and Culture of the Indian People*, 4th edn., Bombay, 1988.

———, *The Age of Imperial Kanauj*, vol. 4 of *The History and Culture of the Indian People*, 2nd edn., Bombay, 1964.

———, 'The Gwalior Prasasti of the Gurjara-Pratīhāra King Bhoja', *EI*, vol. 18, Delhi, repr. 1983, pp. 99–114.

Menon, A.G. and G.H. Schokker, 'The Concept of Rāmārājya in South and North Indian Literature' in *Ritual, State and History in South Asia: Essays in Honour of J.C. Heesterman*, ed. A.W. van Den Hoek, D.H.A. Kolff, M.S. Oort, Leiden, New York and Köln, 1992.

Mill, James, *The History of British India*, vol. I, 1817; Delhi, repr. 1978.

Mirashi, V.V., *Inscriptions of the Kalachuri-Chedi Era* (Corpus Inscriptionum Indicarum, vol. 4, pts. 1-2), Ootacamund, 1955.

———, *Inscriptions of the Śīlāhāras* (Corpus Inscriptionum Indicarum, vol. 6, Delhi, 1977.

Monier-Williams, M., *A Sanskrit-English Dictionary*, Delhi, repr. 1993.

Moraes, G.M., *The Kadamba-kula: A History of Ancient and Medieval Karṇāṭaka*, Bombay, 1931.

Nath, R., 'Rehamāna-Prāsāda: A Chapter on the Muslim Mosque from the Vrksarnava', *Vishveshvaranand Indological Journal*, vol. 15, pt. 2, 1977, pp. 238–44.

Nilakanta Sastri, K.A., *The Pāṇḍyan Kingdom: From the Earliest Times to the Sixteenth Century*, Madras, repr. 1972.

Pant, Mahes Raj, 'Six 15th- and 16th-Century Deeds from Tirhut Recording the Purchase of Slaves', in *Recht, Staat und Verwaltung im Klassischen Indien (The State, the Law, and Administration in Classical India)*, ed. Bernhard Kölver, München, 1997, pp. 158–94.

Parasher, Aloka, *Mlecchas in Early India: A Study in Attitudes towards Outsiders upto AD 600*, Delhi, 1991.

Pingree, D., 'Sanskrit Evidence for the Presence of the Arabs, Jews and Persians in Western India: CA 700-1300, *Journal of the Oriental Institute*, vol. 31.2, 1981–2, pp. 172–82.

Pollock, Sheldon, 'Ramayana and Political Imagination in India', *The Journal of Asian Studies*, vol. 53, no. 2, 1993, pp. 261–97.

Prasad, Pushpa, *Sanskrit Inscriptions of Delhi Sultanate, 1191–1526*, Delhi, 1990.

______, 'The Turushka or Turks in Late Ancient Indian Documents', *Proceedings of the Indian History Congress*, 55th Session, Aligarh, 1994, Delhi, 1995, pp. 170–5.

Ramesh, K..V. and S.P. Tewari, 'An Inscription of Pratīhāra Vatsarāja, Śaka 717', *EI*, vol. 41, Delhi, 1989, pp. 49–57.

Ramesh, K.V., 'A Fragmentary Sarada Inscription from Hund', *EI*, vol. 38, Delhi, 1971, pp. 94–8.

______, *Indian Epigraphy*, vol. I, Delhi, 1984.

Ray, H.P., 'The Yavana Presence in Ancient India', *Journal of the Economic and Social History of the Orient*, vol. 31, 1988, pp. 311–25.

Sachau, Edward C., *Alberuni's India*, vol. 1, London, 1910.

Sadhu Ram, 'Two Inscrpitons from Rampura, Samvat 1664', *EI*, vol. 36, 1965–6, Delhi, 1970, pp. 121–30.

Sandesara, B.J., *Literary Circle of Mahāmātya Vastupāla and its Contribution to Sanskrit Literature*, Bombay, 1953.

Sarma, K.H.V., and T. Krishnamurty, 'Annavarappada Plates of Kataya Vema Reddi', *EI*, vol. 36, pp. 167–70.

Sharma, Arvind, *Studies in 'Alberuni's India'*, Wiesbaden, 1983.

Sharma, R.S., *Aspects of Political Ideas and Institutions in Ancient India*, 3rd revd. edn., Delhi, 1991, Chap. 5.

Shokoohy, M., *Bhadreśvar: The Oldest Islamic Monuments in India*, Leiden, 1988.

Sircar, D.C., 'Veraval Inscription of Chaulukya-Vāghela Arjuna, 1264 AD', *EI*, vol. 34, 1961–2, Delhi, 1963, pp. 141–50.

———, *Select Inscriptions Bearing on Indian History and Civilization,* vol. 2, Delhi, 1982.

———, *Indian Epigraphy,* Delhi, 1965.

———,'Rashtrakuta Charters from Chinchani', *EI,* vol. 32, Delhi, repr. 1987, pp. 55–60.

———, 'Three Grants from Chinchani', *EI,* vol. 32, Delhi, repr. 1987, pp. 61–76.

Smith, David, *Ratnākara's Haravijaya: An Introduction to the Sanskrit Court Epic*, Delhi, 1985.

Stein, M.A., *Kalhaṇa's Rājataranginī: A Chronicle of the Kings of Kashmir,* pt. I, Delhi, repr. 1979.

Sundermann, W., 'An Early Attestation of the Name of the Tajiks', in *Medioiranica* [Proceedings of the International Colloquium organized by the Katholieke Universiteit Leuven from 21 to 23 May 1990 (Leuven, 1990)], ed. W. Skalmowski and A.V. Tongerloo, pp. 163–71.

Talbot, Cynthia, 'Rudrama Devi, the Female King: Gender and Political Authority in Medieval India' in *Syllables of Sky: Studies in South Indian Civilization in Honour of Velcheru Narayana Rao*, ed. David Shulman, Delhi, 1995, pp. 391–430.

———,'Inscribing the Other, Inscribing the Self: Hindu-Muslim Identities in Precolonial India', *Comparative Studies in Society and History,* vol. 37, pt. 4, 1995, pp. 692–722.

Thapar, Romila, 'The Image of the Barbarian in Early India', *Comparative Studies in Society and History,* vol. 13, 1971, pp. 408–36.

———, 'Interpretations of Ancient Indian History', in *Ancient Indian Social History: Some Interpretations*, ed. R. Thapar, Delhi, 1978, pp. 1–25.

———, 'Imagined Religious Communities? Ancient History and the Modern Search for a Hindu Identity', in *Interpreting Early India*, ed. R. Thapar, Delhi, 1992, pp. 60–88.

———, 'Communalism and the Historical Legacy', in *Communalism in India: History, Politics and Culture*, ed. K.N. Panikkar, Delhi, 1991, pp. 17–33.

———, 'The Tyranny of Labels', *Social Scientist 280–81,* vol. 24, nos. 9–10, 1997, pp. 3–23.

Veer, Peter van der, '"The Foreign Hand": Orientalist Discourse in Sociology and Communalism', in *Orientalism and the Postcolonial Predicament: Perspectives on South Asia*, ed. Carol A. Breckenridge and Peter van der Veer, Philadelphia, 1993, pp. 23–44.

Venkataramanayya, N. and M. Somasekhara Sharma, 'Vilasa Grant of Prolaya Nāyaka', *EI*, vol. 32, 1957–8, Delhi, repr. 1987, pp. 239–68.

———, 'Kaleśvaram Inscription of Devaraya I, Śaka 1319', *EI*, vol. 36, pp. 199–202.

Verghese, Anila, *Religious Traditions at Vijayanagara: As Revealed through its Monuments*, Delhi, 1995.

Wagoner, P.B., '"Sultan among Hindu Kings": Dress, Titles and the Islamicization of Hindu Culture at Vijayanagara,' *Journal of Asian Studies*. vol. 55, pt. 4, 1996, pp. 851–80.

Waldman, Marilyn Robinson, 'Toward a Mode of Criticism for Pre-modern Islamicatc Historical Narratives', in *Toward a Theory of Historical Narrative: A Case Study of Perso-lslamicate Historiography*, ed. M.R. Waldman, Colombus, 1980, Chap. I.

Wink, A., 'India and Central Asia: The Coming of the Turks in the Eleventh Century', in *Ritual, State and History in South Asia: Essays in Honour of J.C. Heesterman*, ed. A.W. Van Den Hoek. D.H.A. Kolff and M.S. Oort, Leiden, New York, Köln, 1992, pp. 747–73.

Index